Baptist Wriothesley Noel

Freedom and slavery in the United States of America

Baptist Wriothesley Noel

Freedom and slavery in the United States of America

ISBN/EAN: 9783744741736

Printed in Europe, USA, Canada, Australia, Japan

Cover: Foto ©ninafisch / pixelio.de

More available books at **www.hansebooks.com**

FREEDOM AND SLAVERY

IN THE

UNITED STATES OF AMERICA.

BY

BAPTIST WRIOTHESLEY NOEL.

"He shall judge the poor of the people, he shall save the children of the needy, and shall break in pieces the oppressor. . . . He shall deliver the needy when he crieth; the poor also, and him that hath no helper. . . . He shall redeem their soul from deceit and violence: and precious shall their blood be in his sight."—PSALM lxxii. 4, 12, 14.

LONDON:
JAMES NISBET & CO., 21 BERNERS STREET.
M.DCCC.LXIII.

PREFACE.

I HAVE described in this volume some of the features of society in the Free States and in the Slave States. In another work I shall endeavour to prove the following points:—

1. The slave-holders seceded from the United States without having suffered any wrong.

2. Their secession, being unconstitutional, is a rebellion which the Government ought to suppress.

3. The object of the slave-holders is to extend and perpetuate slavery, with a view to which they have sought to inflict intolerable evils upon their country; and the object of the Government is to save the country, with a view to which it will emancipate the slaves.

4. The Government is likely to suppress the rebellion.

5. The reunion of the two sections of the country will be for the happiness of both.

The objects which I have sought are these:—To do what little I may be able—

To prevent a costly, bloody, and disgraceful war between this country and the United States, which would follow a premature recognition of the South;

To prevent England perpetuating the bondage of four millions of men and women by such a premature recognition;

To promote kind feelings between English and American Christians, who ought to "love as brothers;"

And to make my readers sympathise heartily with the people of the United States in their endeavours to suppress the rebellion.

Although I have written strongly against the slave system, as it deserves, I heartily wish prosperity and happiness to the slave-holders; and believe that these will be secured to them if they will accept emancipation as inevitable, and submit to their Government, with which they have no other cause of quarrel.

CONTENTS.

CHAPTER I.

		PAGE
ON RELIGION AND MORALS IN THE UNITED STATES,	.	1
SECT. I.—Condition of the Working-Classes,	.	2
,, II.—Force of Law, . . .		4
,, III.—The Punishment of Crime, .	.	5
,, IV.—Temperance, ...		6
,, V.—Education, ...		6
,, VI.—Religion, . . .		9
,, VII.—Missions to the Heathen,	. .	29
,, VIII.—The Revival, . . .		34

CHAPTER II.

ON SLAVERY IN THE SLAVE STATES, .	.	54
SECT. I.—The Home Slave Trade,	.	55
,, II.—Slave Labour, . . .		65
,, III.—The Power of the Slave-holder,		74
,, IV.—Profligacy in the Slave States,		82

		PAGE
SECT.	V.—On Cruelty in the Slave States,	91
,,	VI.—Concealment of Crimes,	112
,,	VII.—Opposition to Religious Instruction,	118
,,	VIII.—Effects of Slavery,	135
,,	IX.—Narrative of the Rev. John Sella Martin,	156
,,	X.—Life of Josiah Henson.	170
,,	XL—The will of God respecting Slavery,	194

RECAPITULATION, . . . 208

CONCLUSION, 217

CHAPTER I.

ON RELIGION AND MORALS IN THE UNITED STATES.

THE people of the United States being free, each citizen with respect to his religious opinions is responsible to God alone; and in all other matters may think, speak, and act as he pleases, so long as he does not violate the rights of his fellow-citizens. They have civil and religious liberty in the highest degree, comprehending liberty of speech and action, the freedom of the press, the right to meet, and the right to form associations. Ourselves a free people, we should naturally sympathise with a free people, which is ever ready to unite with us in the defence of freedom against tyranny in every part of the world.

Liberty is so great a blessing to mankind that all who know its value must be sorry to find its fruits bitter in any place where it has been planted. In the United States we have not that source of chagrin. If one great object of government is to do the greatest amount of good to the greatest number, or to allow them to do it for themselves, the American Government has at least that merit.

SECTION I.—CONDITION OF THE WORKING-CLASSES.

In no country of the world are the working-classes so comfortable or so contented as in the older Free States of the Union. Of the New States of the extreme West I do not speak, because, although they are marvels of civilisation, and are fast following the Eastern States, they are scarcely yet settled into orderly societies, under the discipline of established law. The working-classes of New England, New York State, and Pennsylvania are not a mob, but the enlightened citizens of a great republic. By the labour of their hands they have secured for themselves a large share of material comforts; they conduct with intelligence their parish affairs; they support their schools, read their newspapers, discuss the public interests of their country, and elect the representatives who make their laws. "Men are there more equal in their fortune and in their intelligence, more equally strong, than they are in any other country of the world."* "When the people is enlightened, watchful over its interests, and accustomed to attend to them, as in America, the collective force of the citizens will be always more powerful to secure the public welfare than the authority of any government can be. There is not a country in the world where the men make such efforts to secure their social welfare. I do not know a people which has established schools so numerous and so effective; built churches more proportioned to the religious wants

* De Tocqueville, i. 68.

of the inhabitants; or maintained better parish roads. The Union is free and happy as a small nation, glorious and strong as a great one."* "The character of the true American renders him one of the most estimable men in the world. He has little talk, modesty, simple manners, energy, activity; his words are clear, firm, intelligent; his behaviour is delicate; and for all which touches his heart, he has a generosity as beautiful as is to be found on the earth."† "Among the poorest peasants of New England, living on a sterile soil, we see a competency, an order, a cleanliness, a morality unknown among the corresponding classes of Europe. The peasant, here called farmer, has a good house, with a sitting-room cleaner and better furnished than that of the bourgeois in Europe. He studies much, and reads sermons so argumentative that the learned classes alone in other countries would comprehend them. His wife and daughters are ladies, who keep his home in the most perfect order, but who do no work in the fields. They have books in the sitting-room, and know Shakspeare, Milton, Baxter, Bunyan, the English classics, and the best writers of their own country." "An easy modesty, peculiar to the well-educated classes in Great Britain, is almost universal among American women."‡ "America is that country in which of all others in the world the marriage bond is the most respected, and where men have formed the highest and

---

* Ibid., i. 140, 141, 144, 286.
† Rey, L'Amerique Protestante, Paris, 1857, i. 268.
‡ Ibid., i. 278, 299.

most just idea of conjugal happiness." "When after leaving the agitations of the political world the American returns to the bosom of his family, he finds there order and peace. There his pleasures are simple and natural, his joys innocent and tranquil; and as he arrives at happiness by the regularity of his life, he learns thereby to regulate his opinions and his tastes."*

SECTION II.—FORCE OF LAW.

A people so well instructed and so happy are not likely to be lawless; but other causes also give unusual force to the law. Here some among the poorer classes may be tempted to consider the law as their enemy, because it is passed chiefly by the richer classes; but there every man believes the law to be his friend, because he has helped to make it. Some of their laws may be bad, but none can be intended to oppress them, because men do not mean to oppress themselves; as all concur in making the law, all have a parental affection for it. They have passed it for their common welfare, and for the same object they maintain it. If any law, as, for instance, the Morill Tariff, is found to work ill, the people who made can rescind it. Since the "multitudinous sovereign" cannot mean to injure himself, he is always disposed by the aid of experience to correct his mistakes.

On this subject let me again quote De Tocqueville, an author who is as trustworthy for his penetration, as he is estimable for his candour :—

* De Tocqueville, ii. 259.

"Often the European sees in the public officer nothing but force; the American sees in him right. One may say that in America man never obeys man, but always justice and law." *

"The laws in general tend to the good of the greatest number, because they spring from the majority of all the citizens, who may be deceived, but who cannot have an interest against themselves. However vexatious the law may be, the inhabitant of the United States easily submits to it, not only as to the work of the greatest number, but also as to his own work. All classes shew a great confidence in the legislation which governs the country; and, besides, they obey the law because they can change it when it hurts them." †

SECTION III.—THE PUNISHMENT OF CRIME.

As a natural consequence of the general disposition to enforce the law, the country is saved the cost of a vast gendarmerie. Few policemen appear in town or country, yet few criminals escape. "An administrative police," says De Tocqueville, "does not exist, and passports are unknown. Yet I doubt whether there is any country in which crime so rarely escapes punishment." ‡

The prisons of the Union have long been remarkable for their good management. Numbers of them, instead of being confirmed in criminal habits, as often happens elsewhere, through an imperfect gaol discipline, are re-

* Ibid., i. 149.
† Ibid., ii. 125, 143, 144, 145.   ‡ Ibid., i. 151.

formed through their imprisonment; and comparatively few, when liberated, have returned on account of new crimes; because the cells which have been their place of punishment, have proved likewise the means of their conversion.

SECTION IV.—TEMPERANCE.

But the maxim, that prevention is better than cure, is as true as it is trite; and acting on it the Americans have sought to lessen the amount of crime by promoting temperance. Both moral and legislative means have been tried with considerable success. And, although the cheapness of alcoholic drinks still tempts multitudes, especially of the fresh immigrants, great numbers of Americans, by their practice of total abstinence, by their speeches, and by their writings, restrain the evil.

SECTION V.—EDUCATION.

In a country, however, where the majority rule, much more is necessary than the restraint upon vice arising from a knowledge of its consequences. A free people to retain its freedom must be enlightened and virtuous. How else can they respect each other's rights, or know their own interests? This the Americans have up to the present time comprehended, and have therefore paid much attention to popular education.

"The law creates schools in every parish; obliging the parishioners, on pain of heavy fines, to rate themselves for their support. Magistrates must see that parents send their children to the schools, and may fine those who refuse." " I do not think that there is a country in the world where there is so small a proportion of persons who are ignorant. Primary instruction is within the reach of every one, and, as almost all the Americans are in comfortable circumstances, they can easily obtain for themselves the first elements of knowledge."* "Education is open to all in this country; and all, or almost all, are educated. Lately, out of a population of about 60,000 in the State of Massachusetts, only 400, beyond the age of childhood, could not read and write. By returns from 131 towns, presented to the legislature, the number of scholars receiving instruction in those towns is 12,393; the number of persons in those towns, between the ages of fourteen and twenty-one, who are unable to read or write is 58. In the town of Hancock, there are only three persons unable to read and write, and those three are mutes. The general plan of education at the public free schools comprehends grammar, mathematics, geography, history, logic, political economy, moral and natural philosophy. There are at present at Boston 68 free schools, besides 23 Sabbath-schools, in all of which the poorest inhabitant may have his children educated, from the age of four to seventeen, without any expense. In the adjoining State of Connecticut one-third of the population, about 275,000, attend the

* De Tocqueville, i. 47, 66.

free schools. In the New England States, the population of which amounts to about 2,000,000, almost the entire population are educated; that is, can read and write. In the State of New York, 499,434 children, out of a population of 1,900,000, were at the same time attending the schools; that is, a fourth part of the whole population. The appropriations of land for schools in the New States have been regulated by Congress, and their extent is immense. Every township of the new land is divided into 36 sections, each containing a mile square, or 640 acres. One section of every township is appropriated for schools. The facts now stated respecting the number of persons educated and receiving education at schools in the United States will appear the more striking when contrasted with the provision for schools in Great Britain. In England, the number of persons attending schools, instead of being about one-third, as in Connecticut, or one-fourth, as in New York State, is one in sixteen, in Wales one in twenty, in Scotland one in ten. The order and decorum which distinguishes the people of the United States, and the total absence in that country of those who in Britain are designated as the rabble, or the mob, are to be ascribed to the general education of the people."*

"If a traveller asks for their savans, he will find few; but if he counts up those who are ignorant, the American people will seem to him the most enlightened on the earth." "In New England each citizen receives the

* Stuart, i. 310.

elements of knowledge. He learns the doctrines and the proofs of religion, the history of his country, and the chief features of the constitution. In Connecticut and Massachusetts it is very rare to find a man who knows these things imperfectly; and one who is absolutely ignorant of them is a phenomenon. The Americans make no use of the word peasant because they have not the idea. The ignorance of the first ages is gone."*

"I have lived much among the people of the United States, and I cannot say how much I have admired their experience and their good sense."† "The average of persons attending school in all the Union was in 1850, twenty in every hundred. In New England, it is twenty-five in the hundred. In the extreme South, the proportion descends to thirteen in a hundred of the free population. In the North, there is only one illiterate person in four hundred; in the South, one in twelve. Among the European immigrants the proportion of the illiterate is exactly double that of the native Americans."‡

SECTION VI.—RELIGION.

In a well-governed country all pure knowledge is valuable, because it enables a man to understand his obligations to the law, and to foresee the bad consequences of crime. The mere habit of thought is a gain both to the individual who has formed it, and to

* De Tocqueville, ii. 271, 272, 273.
† Ibid., ii. 276. ‡ Roy, ii. 338, 339.

society; because any one who can see the ruin which crime would bring upon him, is less likely to commit it than another is who is blind as well as brutal. Secular knowledge is, however, insufficient to restrain human passion. Under any government religion alone can make a people orderly, contented, and happy; but under no government is religion so necessary to a people as under a democracy. When the people, who rule by their representatives, are passionate, selfish, and unprincipled, they choose leaders like themselves; faction rages against faction; parties, deaf to reason, appeal to force; public and private wrongs render property insecure, and life becomes intolerable; and at length such a people, harassed by evils without number, welcome a military despotism as a shelter from anarchy. What then is the amount of religion in the American people?

The testimony of M. de Tocqueville on this point is explicit:—

"In America religion guides to knowledge, and the observance of the divine law conducts to liberty." "I have said enough to shew the character of Anglo-American civilisation; it is the product of the spirit of religion, and the spirit of liberty." "Liberty sees in religion the companion of her struggles, the cradle of her infancy, the divine source of her rights. She considers religion as the safeguard of morals, and morals as the guarantee of law, and the pledge of her own duration." *

* De Tocqueville, i. 47, 49, 51.

"America is the place where the Christian religion has preserved the most real power over men; and this fact shews how useful and natural it is to man, because the country in which it exercises the greatest power is at the same time the most enlightened and the most free." "In the United States religion does not simply regulate the manners, but also extends its empire over the mind." "Among the Anglo-Americans some profess Christian doctrines because they believe them, others because they fear to seem not to believe them; and so Christianity reigns by the consent of all."*

"Religion ought to be considered as the chief of their political institutions." "I know a European population whose unbelief is only equalled by its brutish ignorance; while in America we see one of the most free and most enlightened peoples in the world fulfilling with ardour the external duties of religion." "Those who disbelieve concealing their unbelief, and those who believe manifesting their faith, a public opinion is created in favour of religion, which is loved, sustained, and honoured." †

The testimony of M. Rey is still more ample:—

"With respect to the Americans, properly so called, and to all the foreigners who, being fused among them, participate in the advantages of that race, *which of all the races under heaven is the most blessed by God*, the first aspect of this class is that of a religious nation."

"It is the country in which, of all others, public

* Ibid., ii. 249, 251.   † Ibid., ii. 252, 257, 267.

opinion is the most decidedly favourable to religion. It is so more than in England, and maintains better whatever is connected with religion, either directly or indirectly, as the rest of the Sabbath." *

The testimony of these upright and intelligent French observers is confirmed by an English lady in the following words:—" The country districts are, however, the most completely under the religious or Puritan influence, and to them the New Englanders point with pride as to a part of the world which is unequalled for its moral beauty. In them religion displays itself as the most powerful of all social elements. There it has planted the church, the college, and the school; it has given free institutions and free speech; it has trained up a noble population of freemen, religious, moral, intelligent, and industrious, dwelling in happy homes, that are the centres of light and love, and which are found only in a land where the Bible is honoured and where the Sabbath is observed. These districts present the remarkable spectacle of a population engaged in peaceful pastoral pursuits, without being dulled by them; tilling the ground which their fathers have tilled before them; educating their children in the fear of God; their sons rising to the highest positions in the country, or carrying to the far West the leaven of religion and morality.

"Virtue, sobriety, industry, reverence for the Sabbath, and love of order, characterise the country population throughout these six States. The people are

* Rey, i. 142, 143.

educated and enlightened: Bunyan's "Pilgrim's Progress," Edwards's Works, and some standard volumes of theology, are to be found in almost the humblest library; and the people are ready to discuss any point of theology with intelligence.

"I take the loveliest village in that surpassingly fair portion of America. It is a village of five thousand people, built on a collection of knolls rising from park-like meadows, through which flow the bright waters of the rushing Connecticut. Beyond the meadow, picturesque hills form an amphitheatre enclosing this gem of Massachusetts; and in whatever direction the eye of the gazer turns, it is satiated with bright visions of material beauty. There are five churches: two Congregational, one Episcopalian, one Baptist, and one Methodist. Their ministers all live in harmony, and engage together in union prayer-meetings. There is no inn or tavern where liquor is sold in the place, and not one policeman or gaol is required for the extensive district.

"The Sabbath morning dawns, and the good people are up betimes to see that their children's lessons are well prepared, and to despatch them to the Sabbath-school: for in New England, children and young persons of all classes and ages attend school, and very frequently the link is only broken by marriage. The Sabbath-school bell rings, and the trampling of many feet is heard; after which there is a profound stillness, broken only by the music of the oriole and the rustle of the humming-bird among the flowers. The sun's rays quiver through the thick trees and dance upon the bright green grass; the cattle repose lazily in the meadows, the mountain shadows lie over the landscape, and man for once does not deface what God has made so beautiful. At ten the bell for meeting rings, and shortly after nearly the whole population is seen moving to the respective churches, while rude country vehicles well laden with human freights pour in along the different lanes. The children, who before this hour have returned from school, invariably accompany their parents, and generally walk according to age, the youngest first, each with Bible and hymn-book in hand, and the parents bring up the rear.

"Every church in that fair village is filled, for all the people are church-goers.

"It is hardly too much to say that these Sabbaths do more than anything else to cement those bonds of family affection which we have never seen stronger than in New England; to make home a charmed spot, ever fresh and ever fragrant; and to keep in active exercise those holy affections that make up the purest of life's enjoyments and smooth so many of life's sorrows. Such is the external influence of religion in the country districts of New England. It is the widespread influence of religion which has made New England, with her severe climate and her barren soil, the most prosperous portion of the Union; which has produced her well-regulated families, her virtuous sons and virtuous daughters. It has been the fashion to sneer at this nation of psalm-singers; but the order-loving and moral population of New England is the best answer to the taunt. . . . . *I believe that the New England States are the most moral, perhaps the most religious portion of the world;* and that in the hearts of their people the love of their sacred faith is equally strong with their attachment to the principles of democratic liberty, the bequest in each instance of their honoured Puritan ancestors."[*]

This religious spirit in the people has led to religious activity. It has built temples for worship, formed Christian churches, maintained pastors, established Sunday schools, distributed Bibles and tracts, and provided preachers for new or neglected districts.

M. Rey thus describes what he saw of their public buildings:—

"The places of worship in the United States are much more attended than those of Europe, and are very numerous."[†] "When I went to Buffalo and Chicago, I was much surprised to see as many chapels and as many good ministers as in the older cities. I found in many American laymen religious fervour, and attention to religion in them all."[‡] "In approaching even the newest cities, I saw the horizon broken by a crowd of church spires; and in moving through the streets, I found these churches to be vast, as varied in style as they were beautiful, and solidly built." "My first impression at the sight of these

---

[*] Aspects of Religion in the United States, by the Author of the "Englishwoman in America." London, 1859.

[†] Rey, i. 117. [‡] Ibid., i. 120.

splendid edifices was surprise at the faith and the generosity of the congregations which furnished the requisite sums. Buffalo has sixty churches and pastors, Chicago fifty, St Louis sixty-four, Cincinnati ninety-one; and these cities are of yesterday."*

These temples are due to the zeal of the churches which have raised them, of the organisation of which M. Rey writes as follows:—" Religious and converted persons settling in any place form themselves into a community of brethren. They are united by a spiritual relationship, as having been born again of one Father who is God, having experienced the work of the Holy Spirit, and believing themselves to be all saved by the same sacrifice—by the death of Christ on the cross. These brethren form an assembly, which is the church of the place, or rather one of the churches. Other persons, not possessing a living Christianity, attend the worship, who, joined to the members of the church, form a larger association called the congregation. All the members of the congregation sustain the worship by their contributions. Those who wish to become members of the church are admitted on the double condition that they make a profession of faith, and that they do not contradict the precepts of the gospel by their lives." †

Churches and Communicants.

In 1857 the number of churches, pastors, and communicants in the principal denominations was as

* Rey, i. 112. † Ibid., ii. 63, 64.

follows, according to M. Rey's classification, who divides the Methodists into two bodies, the Presbyterian and the Episcopalian:—*

	Churches.	Pastors.	Communicants.
Episcopalians, . .	13,341	9,505	1,629,026
Presbyterians, . .	13,753	9,852	1,156,571
Baptists, . . .	14,193	9,080	1,190,609
Total, . .	41,287	28,437	3,976,206

This is a result which, when we recollect the comparatively scanty supply of churches, pastors, and communicants in the Slave States, shews that there must be much religious zeal in the Free States.

Sunday-Schools.

Almost every church has its Sunday-school. "They never build a chapel without adding a school-room capable of holding all the children of the congregation; and there each Sunday the children are collected for instruction in the Bible. These schools have twenty or thirty teachers, and here several hundreds of thousands of instructed and pious Americans teach more than two millions and a half of children each Sabbath."†

Still, as there were in 1850 five millions of children between five and fifteen years of age, nearly half of them were left without Sabbath instruction. This

* Ibid., ii. 73.   † Ibid., i. 103, 104.

shews the need there was for the existence of the American Sunday-School Union. The report of that Society, in May 1855, gave the following results:—

"The agents of our Society, without speaking of what has been done by others, have organised, within the year, 2440 Sunday-schools, where none existed before; they have induced more than 16,000 persons to become teachers; and they have brought to the schools 97,000 children. The Society has had in its service during the year 324 missionaries, 256 of whom are students of theology, who have consecrated their vacation to this work." *

General use of the Word of God.

By all these pastors, churches, and Sunday-school teachers, the Word of God is studied, believed, venerated, taught; and so it forms the faith of the nation. As might be expected, it is therefore largely distributed in the country. The American Bible Society of New York has published more than one copy of the Bible or Testament for every three inhabitants of the United States. It has 2000 auxiliaries, with 4000 depôts; and its colporteurs hawk the Bible through the country. In the year 1854, it issued 815,000 volumes; and in 1855, 749,000. Its receipts in 1854 were $346,000; and the contributions of the Free States alone, for the distribution of the Bible, in 1858-9, were $715,620.†

* Rey, i. 105, 106.   † Ibid., i. 83-89; 341.

Religious Tracts.

The Americans have not been less active in the distribution of tracts. The Tract Society has published 1540 tracts, and 408 volumes. During its 30 years of existence it has issued 10,000,000 volumes, and 158,000,000 tracts. During the year 1856, its issues were 1,070,000 volumes, and 13,127,000 tracts; and 695 colporteurs were in its service, who visited 639,193 families.* The whole amount of contributions in the Free States for religious tracts was in 1858–9, $129,690.† Two of the periodicals published by the Tract Society have obtained an unexampled success. The *American Messenger*, a monthly paper, has reached a circulation of 200,000 copies; and the *Child's Paper* has now 300,000 subscribers. We have no instances of success like these.‡ Further, the religious papers and reviews publish about 34,000,000 of copies annually;§ and in every great city there is also a Young Men's Christian Association, the members of which are engaged in doing good.

By these and other means the Christians of America endeavour to render their nation a Christian nation; notwithstanding the large accession of European immigrants, who bring with them, too often, complete indifference to religion, or positive unbelief. Let us hear M. Rey:—"What is it then which preserves this interesting nation from religious indifference? Millions of immigrants flow in from Europe ignorant of the

* Ibid., i. 93, 94.   † Ibid., 341.   ‡ Ibid., 98, 99.   § Ibid., 99.

gospel." "European lepers form a great part of the stock of vice and irreligion in the United States. Irishmen and Germans commit the murders of New York, fill the prisons, and furnish the drunkards." "A mass of irreligious Germans, 30,000 or 40,000, are accumulated at St Louis, where they have some Rationalist pastors, of whom they make moreover very little use." "The 'little flock' knows all this perfectly, and strives against the danger." "It is astonishing to see the boldness of the Americans in industry, speculation, war, commerce; but nowhere is it greater than in the way in which they advance religion. So, although the American nation, as descended from Adam, has been sin-stricken, still Christianity advances there in spite of difficulties which would arrest it elsewhere. That immense immigration of European Philistines, those savages from the banks of the Rhine who roar at the name of religion, of Christ, of morality, are restrained, and by degrees reclaimed. They do not succeed here in turning public opinion against Christian doctrine, as is the case in Europe; but, on the contrary, the public favour still rests more or less with religious men and with the cause of religion." *

Notwithstanding the extraordinary increase of population in the Western States, "those countries are so well furnished with chapels, ministers, and schools, that they are not inferior in that respect to the old Eastern States. They contain, indeed, here and there,

* Rey, L 100, 110, 111, 102, 119.

compact masses of European settlers, who live in a state of materialism painfully contrasted with that of the Americans; but even this army of unbelievers is broken in upon by American activity."* "God has provided that unheard-of needs are met with a generosity beyond all example. In England it has been found that there are sittings in places of worship for 57 in 100; but in the United States, there are sittings for 61 in 100 of the population." †

In nearly the whole of New England "*the entire population has submitted to a religious influence, attends worship, supports it by its contributions, and renders homage to Christianity by its moral conduct.*"‡ In New York and in the great cities of the West, the population which attends no worship and has no religion "is entirely composed of foreigners from Europe." "The poison of an antichristian education is brought from beyond the seas. But let the principle of these free churches only act a certain time, and these brutal masses of Irishmen and Germans will bless their new country for having given them the bread of the soul with a liberality of which no land offers so fair an example." § "It is a great thing to have missionaries by thousands in a country already civilised. Churches which, besides their own expenses, can furnish 3577 missionaries for poorer districts, at a cost of 4,000,000 of francs, must not be taxed with inertness." ‖ The contributions of the Free States for this object in 1859 were $197,630.¶

* Ibid., ii. 83.   † Ibid., 84.   ‡ Ibid., 85.
§ Ibid., 85, 86.   ‖ Ibid., 90.   ¶ Holper, 341.

To an English member of Parliament who said lately that the Americans of the Northern States were the refuse and scum of Europe, the *New York Evening Post* replied, "Now let us see who are Mr R.'s blackguards. They are the scoundrels who have founded in a single county more common schools than are maintained in the whole State of Virginia,—who have built more churches in a single city than stand in many a Southern State,—who have public libraries in little towns which outnumber all the books to be found in many a Southern capital,—who fill up the great granaries of the West, and who build and man the immense commercial fleets of the East,—who pay their debts, and who by industry have so increased the aggregate of the public wealth, while equalising its distribution, that here and there considerable towns may be pointed out without a pauper."—*Daily News*, Sept. 29. What a high tone there must be in that society which can raise such fruits as these from persons whom Europe had degraded into "scum and refuse!"

Here let me add two other valuable testimonies. The first is from a French Catholic:—

"It would be difficult to find in any part of the earth societies morally superior to those of Vermont, Massachusetts, Rhode Island, New Hampshire. The majority of those composing them are conscious of their freedom and of their worth; instruction is general; the spirit of invention is active to the last degree; a love of the fine arts is developing; every commendable undertaking is supported with unexampled generosity; progress in all things has become the general end. And what freedom has produced in this corner of the land, she will doubtless produce through the vast Anglo-Saxon republic, when the crime of slavery is expiated, and the black, delivered at last from his chains, shall be able to press in his hands that of his former master." *

The second is from my friend M. G. Fisch, a faithful Protestant pastor in Paris:—

"A traveller who studies America begins to understand it as soon as he learns the place which is there occupied by religion. There he sees the least village piercing the horizon by its church spires. The churches, in number more than forty thousand, have been built and are maintained by private contributions. Hence he learns that religion must there have extraordinary vitality, to have won for itself the highest place, though exposed to so many adverse circumstances. There religion is more free, more active, and more influential than it has ever been in any part of the world. That nation, indeed, whose ancestors sacrificed the world for God, exchanging the enjoyments of their country for a desert in which they might follow conscience, has been formed by it. The Evangelical Church is composed of the communicants of four or five great denominations, in which the doctrine and the practice of the gospel have been preserved in their purity.

* M. Elisée Reclus. *Revue des Deux Mondes*, Jan. 1, 1861. In Ludlow, p. 315.

"The Presbyterians call themselves the spinal marrow of the United States. Although that pretension is lofty, it is well founded. When we join to them the Congregationalists, who are of the same family, they reach the number of 8000 churches and 950,000 communicants who have preserved strong Puritan traditions. The Episcopalian is the most fashionable church. But while the highest classes shelter themselves under its care, we also find within it the most elevated spirituality. The Methodist and the Baptist systems have long been the religious forms preferred by the artisans and by the poor negroes. These two denominations have shared the task of evangelising the slaves, and they have admirably succeeded. If any one describes the Southern blacks as hordes of savages, or troops of wild beasts ready to spread round them devastation and death, he knows that he speaks falsely. A great proportion of them profess piety. We may thus explain their conduct during this conflict, from which they are expecting their emancipation. In general the more intelligent negroes are Baptists. I was surprised at Louisville, Kentucky, to find the slaves divided into two parties—the aristocracy, which was Baptist, and the common people, who were Methodists. The Baptists and Methodists are the most numerous denominations in the United States. The Methodists have 16,000 churches, served by 12,200 pastors, with 2,000,000 communicants. One of its sections—the Methodist Episcopal Church of the Northern States—built in 1860, 450 churches and 134 manses. A year ago it possessed 9754 temples and 103 seminaries, with 600 professors and 25,000 scholars. The Baptists are less numerous; but they have about 11,000 churches, 10,600 pastors, and 1,214,000 communicants. To these five denominations we must add the Lutheran, which has 1600 churches. There was a time when Boston, the Athens of the New World, was Unitarian; but the Unitarians are now a minority: nine-tenths of the population of Massachusetts belong to the different evangelical denominations, and there are not more than three hundred Unitarian churches in all America.

"The unity of Protestantism is nowhere more evident than in this country. It is chiefly seen in their evangelical doctrine and morality. But doctrine and morals are religion. In this point of view, America is a powerful apology for Christianity. There we find not less than forty-four thousand evangelical churches belonging to six distinct groups. They own no external authority, and religious thought among them is perfectly independent; and yet the great doctrines of the gospel are taught within them with as much clearness as force. They profess in common these vital doctrines: the Divine inspiration of the Scriptures, the fall of man, the Trinity, redemption by the expiatory sacrifice of the Saviour, salvation by free grace, justification by faith, and regeneration by the Holy Spirit. No one asks admission to a church without believing himself to be really a Christian, and all these churches exercise discipline upon their members.

This unity is not less evident from the spirit which animates that vast body. The different denominations have their journals, which consecrate a special article to each of the other churches; and the friendliness by which they are marked forms a painful contrast with the pugnacious habits of European ecclesiastical journalism. Their one business is unitedly to fight for the truth.

"Nowhere can be found so distinguished a body of pastors. They march not only at the head of their churches, but at the head of the nation. It has been remarked that all the illustrious men of the United States have been sons or grandsons of clergymen. There are few blots in this picture. Nothing is more rare in America than a worldly or immoral pastor.

"Free from all shackles, and directed by the most enlightened and the most respected clergy in the world, the American Church naturally exercises a prevailing influence in the destiny of the nation. It reigns without control over that society, so living, so energetic, and so jealous of its rights. The *élite* of the nation believe, theoretically at least, in the truth of Christianity. The American Sabbath is not less strict, though less Judaising than that of Scotland, and family worship is practised everywhere. A New York society has enlisted thousands of persons from the highest classes, who visit monthly all the families of that immense city, to offer them religious tracts. The Society for the Observation of the Lord's Day at New York strives vigorously with a formidable league composed of six thousand Irish and German public-house keepers.

"The liberality of American Christians is admirable. The average salary of pastors is twenty-five hundred francs. In 1850 there were thirty-six thousand churches, now there are forty-eight thousand. Reckoning one pastor to a church, the annual cost of worship is one hundred and twenty millions, which is three times that of France; and every year about twelve hundred new churches are built, at the cost of about forty millions. It is impossible to see without admiration the Bible-house of New York, containing five hundred windows,—a palace raised to the honour of the Divine Book.

"American manners are the result of strong religious convictions, which have penetrated into the habits, sentiments, and inner life of the nation. With the exception of Washington and New York, which are almost European, one breathes in America a moral atmosphere entirely unknown in our old world.

"Private and public education are completed by the Sunday-school. The United States could not subsist as they now are without the Sunday-schools. Three millions of scholars and four hundred thousand teachers form an army which is perfectly organised. All the *élite* of the churches beg as a favour to be made teachers. Some congregations contain two hundred or three hundred teachers. The children love the Sunday-school passionately. Their eyes sparkle when one speaks of it.

"The trait which strikes a stranger the moment that he lands in that New World is its intelligence. The Yankees are the most inventive people on the earth. Its inventive genius is explained by the great amount of knowledge which circulates through every rank of society. But we must not think that in America intellect dries up the heart. If that people produces machines to excess, it is profoundly sensitive to poetic impressions. God is beyond doubt calling it to destinies as great in the world of mind as in that of matter. If we except the Irish immigrants, we do not meet in the rural parts of the six (New England) States more than one class. Some are richer than others, some are agriculturists, some bankers, and some magistrates, but all are instructed and enlightened. That variety of the human race which is called peasant is not known there. There are whole counties in which there is not found a single pauper. It is impossible to imagine anything more happy than the population placed on the enchanting banks of the beautiful river Connecticut. They are healthy, vigorous, active, prosperous; and they acknowledge with thankfulness that they have received the best lot which can be enjoyed here below."*

We may now see why the working classes in New England are so happy. It is not their fertile territory which is the cause; because those States are fully peopled, and their lands need as much skilful husbandry as ours do; but the cause is the amount of knowledge and of religious principle among them. Their

* Les Etats-Unis en 1861, par Georges Fisch. Paris, 1862.

schools are good, their places of worship are numerous, they have a large supply of pious pastors, each church has its effective Sunday-school, the Bible is known and read by more than half the population; evangelical tracts, magazines, and journals, pervade the whole country; and, as De Tocqueville says, "*it is the place in all the world where religion has retained the greatest power over men's minds.*"* Nor must we exclude the other Free States from this description. All of the older States follow close the example of the New Englanders; and even the hardy and adventurous populations which fell the forests, or spread over the prairies of the extreme West, form schools where they have no settled ministers; and receive visits from large numbers of colporteurs, evangelists, and home missionaries, who bring to them a knowledge of the gospel.

SECTION VII.—MISSIONS TO THE HEATHEN.

Further, through the grace given to them, they have done much, though their own population has been growing so rapidly, to promote the knowledge of the Lord Jesus Christ among the heathen. For the two hundred millions of idolaters in India, whom the providence of God has placed under our care, we have done too little. Numbers among us take no interest in their conversion; and although Jesus has said to His disciples, "Go ye into all the world, and preach the gospel to every creature: he that believes and is bap-

* " L'Amerique est le lieu du monde où la réligion Chrétienne a conservé le plus de véritable pouvoir sur les âmes."—ii. 249.

tized shall be saved," some openly despise the attempts which a few zealous men among us make to save them. Our government, which ought to be impartial in its rule towards its subjects of every creed, and which very wisely abstains from acting itself in any missionary capacity, dishonours, as I think, both our Creator and itself, when it professes *neutrality* between truth and falsehood, between impure superstitions and the doctrines of Christ, between the worship of God and a base idolatry. But as if that were not irreligious enough, it sinks beneath neutrality. It forbids its schoolmasters to allow the Word of God to be read in their schools, when their scholars wish to read it; and while its Mohammedan and Hindoo servants may preach both the Koran and the Shasters, its Christian servants may not speak to the people of Christ. Two hundred millions of idolaters and Mohammedans will therefore perish in their corruption and their enmity to God, unless they are taught by missionaries. To a few British evangelists who are prosecuting this gigantic undertaking, protected indeed by law, but often frowned on by men in power, our American brethren have lent their effective aid. The only instructors who were teaching the natives to be faithful to the Queen in Meerut, when the mutiny broke out there, were Americans. Scarcely one native Christian, perhaps not one, joined the rebellion. Each one of them, on the contrary, was a hindrance to it, and is now a stone in the breakwater on which, in future, sedition will break its waves. At this defence of order the Americans were working as hard as our own zealous countrymen. When the revolt began, Lahore and the Punjab, which, under the vigorous administration of Sir John Lawrence, sent its Sikh levies to recover Delhi, owed much to Americans. For while he, with his coadjutors, Montgomery, Edwardes, Nicholson, and others, whose names have added lustre to our country, was promoting its material prosperity by his strong and equitable rule, Americans, under his protection, were labouring to convert it to Christ. Descending the Ganges, we come to Cawnpore, where the blood of American martyrs, who had been preaching Christ at Futtehghur, was mingled with that of our countrymen by Nana Sahib. Oude, which is now pacified and prospering under British rule, has received only three or four British missionaries for its five millions of inhabitants, and its only other Christian teachers are American. No less upon both shores of the Indian peninsula do these energetic men from New England aid us in our necessary work. Near Bombay the province of Aurungabad is studded with their stations, where the praises of God are sung by Mahrattas, whom they have reclaimed from a fatal idolatry. And, in the extreme south-west, round Madura, they have reaped spiritual harvests as large as those which God has given to British missionaries in Tinnevelly, Neyoor, and Nagercoil.

In Jaffnapatam, their efforts have been so successful that every British missionary in Ceylon has been animated by their zeal as well as instructed by their wisdom. On the eastern coast of the Bay of Bengal, they have been labouring almost alone. The great valley of Assam has no Christian teachers but those who have been sent thither by American Christians; their zeal alone has given the gospel to the capital city of Burmah; and in Arracan, Pegu, and Tenasserim, they have preached the Lord Jesus with such aid from the Holy Spirit, that thousands of Karens have become His true disciples, many of whom are in their turn labouring to make Him known to their countrymen.

For this unwearying charity to our Hindoo and Karen fellow-subjects we are immensely their debtors. God has blessed them as much as He has us in this work of faith, and on one account they are more useful than we are. For while Mohammedans and Brahmins may ascribe our zeal to selfishness, believing that we desire by subverting their faith to rivet their fetters, they can find no such explanation of the American zeal which strengthens the dominion of a people separated from America by three thousand miles.

So much have these missions interested the Americans in the establishment of our rule in India, that while some French papers, guided perhaps by their wishes, pronounced our Indian empire lost and our cause hopeless, as some Englishmen now speak of the cause of the Union, the Americans were almost as generally anxious to see the rebellion extinguished as we were ourselves. When one noble British soldier fell after another, they wept them as we did; specially when Havelock died under exertions too great for an iron frame and a heroic spirit, the flags half-mast high in every American port told how they sympathised in our loss. At that time our Christian brethren then felt that our cause was theirs: and though we had a territory to recover far larger than the Cotton States, and a much smaller army with which to recover it, their sympathy with our cause would never allow them to doubt of our success.

Not less they have been our allies along the coast of China. Each of those five ports which were first opened to European commerce has now its American mission; and when the gospel shall have saved the millions who crowd the fertile banks of the Hoangho and the Yang-tze-kiang, American diplomacy and American preaching will have had their full share in the great transformation. At Canton, Fuchou, Amoy, Shanghai, and Ning-po, Chinamen now hear from Americans of salvation through the atoning blood of Jesus; and if their churches at home grow in grace, we may be sure that other brave evangelists, recruiting their sacred band, will soon carry the glad tidings to the foot of the great Thibet chain. So they labour with us as brothers, to give our Redeemer glory among the swarming populations of Eastern Asia.

Coming into Western Asia, where the Koran has done its deadliest work, we find them working with equal intelligence, faith, and charity to raise the dispirited and demoralised Christian churches of the Turkish empire. At Beyrout and Sidon, among the Nestorians, among the Armenians of Asia Minor, and in Constantinople itself, are they renewing, after the lapse of eighteen centuries, the apostolic triumphs of Paul. Patiently, perseveringly, and at length with great success, they have laboured where others feared to enter, or fainted after entering. Especially now are the Armenians so far rewarding their zeal, that evangelical churches of that people are beginning to send forth native evangelists to regenerate the decrepit East, to rescue those decayed denominations from deadly superstitions, and to renew the faith and the fervency of apostolic times.

SECTION VIII.—THE REVIVAL.

Christians so devout and so active in doing good were likely both to perceive and to lament any measure of religious declension in their churches. And in the year 1857, when various causes had brought upon them this mischief, some began earnestly to wish for a revival. God, who is the author of spiritual life, can alone reinvigorate the faith and love of Christians when they have suffered decay. From Him, therefore, they sought this blessing; and, in September of that year, various prayer-meetings began to be held for this purpose.

The first united prayer-meeting in New York was held September 13, at 12 o'clock, in a lecture-room of the North Dutch Church, Fulton Street, by six Christian men of five different denominations. At the second meeting, September 30, twenty persons were present. At the next meeting, October 7, thirty attended. The next day, October 8, a large number gathered together; and then it was agreed that a meeting should be held there at the same hour daily. "This meeting was one of uncommon fervency in prayer, of deep humility, and of great desire that God would glorify Himself in the outpouring of His Spirit upon them."* On the 9th, a large number again met, who found the place "the very gate of heaven." By the 14th, the numbers had increased to a hundred. And on that day many were "brought under a conviction of sin, and were seeking an interest in Christ."† I shall now continue this narrative in the words of Dr Prime:—

"During the first month of these meetings, many city pastors, and many laymen, belonging to the churches of New York and Brooklyn, had been into one or more of these meetings, and had been warmed by the holy fire. And as the sparks from the burning building are borne to kindle other fires, so these carried the fire to their own churches.

"Not only in the Fulton Street meeting was prayer made, but morning prayer-meetings began to be established in different churches. The Broome Street Church was one of the first to open a morning prayer-meeting. Other churches followed, both in New York and Brooklyn, without any preconcert or any knowledge of each other's movements. In the second month of the Fulton Street meetings, several morning daily prayer-meetings were in existence. The place of

* The Power of Prayer, by Dr Prime, p. 10.   † Ibid.

prayer was a most delightful resort; and the places of prayer multiplied, because men were moved to prayer. They wished to pray. They felt impelled by some unseen power to pray. They felt the pressure of the call to prayer. So a place of prayer was no sooner opened, than Christians flocked to it, to pour out their supplications together. Christians of both sexes, of all ages, of different denominations, without the slightest regard to denominational distinctions, came together, on one common platform of brotherhood in Christ; and in the bonds of Christian union sent up their united petitions to the throne of the heavenly Giver.

"The early dawn of the revival was marked by love to Christ, love for all His people, love of prayer, and love of personal effort. Never in any former revival, since the days of the first Christians, was the name of Christ so honoured, never so often mentioned, never so precious to the believer. Never was such ardent love to Him expressed. Never was there so much devotedness to His service. The whole atmosphere was love. It is not strange, then, that those who so loved Him, should love His image wherever and in whomsoever they saw it. It was a moral necessity. The union of Christians was felt. It needed no professions. Hence there was no room for sectarian jealousies. It was felt that all Christians had a right to pray; all were commanded to pray; all ought to pray. And if all wished to pray, and pray together, who should hinder?

"This union of Christians in prayer struck the unbelieving world with amazement. It was felt that this was prayer. This love of Christians for one another, and this love of Christ, this love of prayer and love of souls, this union of all in prayer, whose names were lost sight of, disarmed all opposition, so that not a man opened his mouth in opposition. On the contrary, the conviction was conveyed to all minds, that this truly is the work of God. The impenitent felt that Christians loved them: that their love of souls made them earnest. The truth now commended itself to every man's conscience in the sight of God. They felt that this was not the work of man, but the work of God. They were awed by a sense of the divine presence in the prayer-meeting, and felt that this was holy ground. Christians were very much humbled. Impenitent men saw and felt this. They felt that it was awful to trifle with the place of prayer. . . . . And men *prayed* in the prayer-meeting, as if they expected God would hear and answer prayer. All these convictions, combined, made almost all classes of men approachable on the subject of religion. It was not difficult to get access to their hearts. God thus prepared the way for their conviction and conversion. Before the close of the second month of the daily prayer-meeting, the two lower lecture-rooms had been thrown open, and both were filled immediately. Yet so gradually and unostentatiously had all this widespread religious interest arisen, that one meeting for prayer scarcely had any knowledge of what was doing in any other. The religious interest was now rapidly on the increase, and was extending itself to all parts of the country. Many men of business from abroad, coming to New York on business, would enter into the noonday prayer-meetings and become deeply impressed; and go to their respective homes to tell what the Lord was doing in New York.

"When we come to the history of the third month of prayer, what a change we find rapidly taking place, not only in the city, but all over the land! It was everywhere a revival of prayer. It was not prayer-meetings in imitation of the Fulton Street prayer-meetings. Those that say so, or think so, greatly err. God was preparing His glorious way over the nation. It was the desire to pray. The same power that moved to prayer in Fulton Street, moved to prayer elsewhere. The same characteristics that marked the Fulton Street meeting, marked all similar meetings. The Spirit of the Lord was poured out upon these assemblages, and it was this that made the places of prayer all over the land places of great solemnity and earnest inquiry. Men did not doubt—could not doubt —that God was moving in answer to prayer. It was this solemn conviction that silenced all opposition— that awakened the careless and stupid—that encouraged and gladdened the hearts of Christians—causing a general turning to the Lord.

"At the end of the fourth month the Fulton Street prayer-meeting occupied the three lecture-rooms in the consistory building, and all were filled to their utmost capacity. The three lecture-rooms at the old Dutch church had become filled to overflowing, one after the other, until no sitting room or standing room was left, and scores, and perhaps hundreds, had to go away, unable even to get into the halls. How noticeable is one fact, and it must be noticed, in order that we may see that 'the excellency of the power is of God.' There had been no eloquent preaching, no energetic and enthusiastic appeals, no attempts to rouse up religious interest. All had been still, solemn, awful. The simple fact, the great fact, was, the people were moved to *prayer*. The people demanded a place to *pray*. So noiseless was this work of grace, that one portion of the community did not know what any other portion were doing in the matter. Instead of devising plans, and executing them, to stir up the community, the whole community, as one man, seemed to be already roused. The daily prayer-meeting was not the means of the feeling, but the mere expression of it. Never, since the days of Pentecost, was such a state of the general Christian heart and mind; and never, since the world was made, was there such an important epoch. The more we go into the facts of it, the more is the mind filled with adoring wonder and amazement at the stupendous importance and extent of it. Every movement in it seemed following, not leading; not creating, but following the developments of a plan already marked out; the end by no means seen from the beginning, and no part of the plan seen but only as it was unfolded, from day to day, by Him who devised it all.

"This revival is to be the precursor of greater and more wonderful things, which are yet to be revealed in the providence of God. What these are we cannot tell. But 'coming events cast their shadows before.' As this is a law in the kingdoms of nature, providence, and grace, so we may unhesitatingly conclude that, however eventful may be the interests of the present times, we shall 'see greater things than these.'

"Early in February it was felt that these retreating hundreds, who came to the place of prayer in Fulton Street, and could not get in, must be accommodated elsewhere. The old John Street Methodist Church, only one square removed, was thrown open for noon prayer-meetings by our Methodist brethren, and the whole body of the church was immediately filled every day, at noon, with business men, who would come, and did come, to pray. The galleries, too, were occupied all round the church chiefly by ladies. No denominational element seemed to be prominent one above another. No one could have told who had come in, a stranger, from the character of the meeting, whether it was held in a Methodist, Baptist, Presbyterian, or Congregationalist church, or that of any other denomination. It was found at once that the audience-room was insufficient, and the basement lecture-room was opened and immediately filled. It was estimated that two thousand persons attended upon these services daily. There were now five noonday services—three in the Fulton Street Church, and two in the John Street Church; and yet hundreds would go away, unable to get into any of them, so much were men moved to prayer. Answers to prayer came down speedily, and multitudes were now turning to God.

"On the 17th of March, Burton's old theatre, in Chambers Street, was opened by a number of merchants in that vicinity for a noonday prayer-meeting. This was thronged to excess after the first meeting. Half-an-hour before the time to commence the services, the old theatre would be crowded to its utmost capacity, in every nook and corner, with most solemn audiences. The streets and all means of access were blocked up before the hour of prayer commenced, and hundreds would stand in the street during the hour. This continued to be the case until the building was required by the United States courts, when the further use of it for prayer-meetings ceased.

"Immediately a store (No. 69 Broadway, second story) was procured and comfortably fitted up for the purpose of prayer-meetings. The room was twenty-five by a hundred feet, and this from day to day was filled, and the exercises were solemn beyond description. Other meetings were established in almost every part of New York and the surrounding cities. The great features of all these meetings were union, and prayer, and corresponding effort.

"A careful inquiry in regard to the facts convinces us that not less than one hundred and fifty meetings for prayer in this city and Brooklyn were held daily at the time of which we are now writing, *all*, without one single exception, partaking of the *same general character*.

"In February, Philadelphia established a noon-day prayer-meeting, commenced at first in a church in Fourth Street, but soon removed to Jaynes' Hall. Soon the entire accessible places were filled,—floor, platform, galleries, boxes, aisles, and office. Never were there scarcely on the face of the earth such meetings as those in Jaynes' Hall. The death of the Rev. Dudley A. Tyng, of the Episcopal Church, a prominent leader in these meetings, gave an impetus to the work. And here again we find Bishop M'Ilvaine lending his influence by his presence and his prayers and preaching.

"The work spread from Jaynes' Hall all over the city. Prayer-meetings were established in numerous places, in public halls, concert-rooms, engine and hose companies' houses, and in tents, till the whole city seemed pervaded with the spirit of prayer.

"Prayer-meetings almost simultaneously were established in all parts of the land, both in city and country. The fervour of this awakened religious interest had become intense at the end of the fourth month of the meetings, and towards the close of the first month of the current year the newspapers, both secular and religious, in all parts of the country, speak of an 'unwonted revival of religion' in all quarters, far and near everywhere men were crowding to the meetings, and the spirit with which they were impressed seemed to animate the whole land. The northern, middle, western, and southern States were moved as by one common mighty influence.* The spirit of the revival spread everywhere, and seemed to permeate every nook and corner of the great republic. The subjects of the revival included all classes—the high and the low, the rich and the poor, the learned and the ignorant. The most hopeless and forbidding were brought under its mighty power. From the highest to the lowest in society, the trophies of God's power and grace were made. Persons of the most vicious and abandoned character, supposed to be beneath and beyond the reach of all religious influence, were brought to humble themselves like little children at the foot of the cross. Christians were themselves astonished and overwhelmed at those displays of divine mercy. They felt that God was saying to them anew and by a providential revelation—'Before they call I will answer, and while they are yet speaking I will hear.' 'Open thy mouth wide, and I will fill it.' Christians became emboldened to ask great things, and expect great things. Never before, in modern times certainly, was there such asking in prayer—such believing in prayer; and never such answers to prayer. The spectacle of such universal confidence in God was without a parallel. It appeared in all prayers. It appeared in all addresses. It appeared in all conversation. It spread from heart

* "It is a noteworthy fact that the revival has scarcely penetrated into the Southern States; and the earnest and persevering prayers which have ascended from Southern Christians have not been answered by any marked outpouring of the Holy Spirit."—*Aspects of Religion in the United States*, p. 102.

to heart. There was humility, and yet there was a cheerful, holy boldness in the spirit and temper of the religious mind, and duty was attempted with the expectation of success. It seemed to be upon all hearts as if written with the pen of a diamond: 'My soul, wait thou only upon GOD, for my expectation is from Him.'

"Is it wonderful, then, that we should find that this state of heart and mind in all praying places and praying circles, this earnest asking, this humble confiding, this far-reaching faith, should be followed by such a work of grace as the modern Christian world has never seen?

"Christians began to feel that they had entered upon a new era of faith and prayer, and is it wonderful that this new joy and hope spread with vast rapidity over the land? The numbers converted were beyond all precedent. The great revival in the times of Wesley, Whitfield, Edwards, and the Tennants, was marked by powerful preaching; the present, by believing, earnest praying.

"In New England, the present great revival commenced almost simultaneously in many cities, villages, and townships. Since the former 'great awakening,' as it was commonly denominated, and just referred to, nothing had borne any comparison to the present religious interest. *This* great awakening surpassed the *former* in all its aspects. It entered into all the framework of society, and permeated everywhere the masses. Christians gathered for prayer, and asked for large measures of the Holy Spirit to be poured out upon them; and the Spirit was sent down in copious effusions in answer to prayer. The prayer-meeting would be established in lecture-rooms and vestries, and all at once it would be found that scarcely could the largest churches contain the hundreds who would come up to the house of GOD to pray. Nothing was thought of or demanded but a place in which to pray. Conversions multiplied, so that there was, after a little, no attempt to compute their numbers. In some towns nearly all the population became, as was believed, true and faithful followers of Christ. The number of converted men and women constituted a new element of power. New voices were daily heard imploring the divine blessing on the work, and the moral transformation of those remaining impenitent. The day was breaking that should be gilded by the rays of a brighter sun than had ever shone upon the moral and religious world before. This was believed. It *is* believed now.

"This present revival is ever treated with respect, even by those who have no sympathetic interest in it. Opposition is disarmed. Ridicule is not attempted; and if it be, it is soon rebuked, and abandoned for very shame.

"That there is enthusiasm—a well-regulated and joyful enthusiasm—we are most happy to admit. No right mind can contemplate great changes and great events for *good* without enthusiasm.

"What mighty results are to be realised in the bearings of this work on the social, the political, the religious character of this nation? No mind can think of them without being impressed with their overwhelming importance.

"Nothing but the influence of a deep and all-pervading earnest piety can save this from the fate of all past republics. The tide of corruption must be rolled backward.

"This was everywhere felt. The place of prayer was *the* place to get the help we needed. Men rushed to the place of prayer with high resolves, and with weighty demands to ask great things of GOD. And men rejoiced with unbounded joy when they saw what God was doing. Why should not a holy enthusiasm be enkindled? It was kindled, and God be praised!

"One of the most deeply interesting characteristics of this revival has been its catholicity.

"The 'union prayer-meeting' is now a *type*. It represents what has never been so well represented before in modern days: that among all Christians there are elements of coalescence and harmony; that there is a union deeper down, and which underlies all external 'unions.' Otherwise the 'union prayer' would be a misnomer. But now the name only suggests a meaning which fills all hearts with joy and gladness. The reality of this union is proved from the fact that in all our large towns and cities, the numbers attending upon the union prayer-meeting far surpassed the numbers attending any one church in the same place. So it has been in New York. So it has been in Philadelphia, and all our large cities. Thus proving that it is really what it professes to be—a union meeting. Thousands go without ever raising the question whom they are to meet, or to what church-organisation they belong.

"The preaching of the gospel has been signally blessed, in the edification of saints and the conviction and conversion of sinners. The attendance on the sanctuary has been largely increased, and pastors have preached with energy, distinctness, and hope; exhibiting the truths of the gospel with great clearness and fulness; declaring the whole counsel of God. And it has pleased Him to put honour upon His word; making it in thousands of instances the acknowledged instrument of bringing lost men to the Saviour.

"In the autumn of this same year the large hall of the Cooper Institute, seating 2500 persons, was opened for religious worship on Sabbath evenings, with preaching by the Rev. J. L. Cuyler, pastor of the Market Street Church. It was immediately filled to overflowing, and thousands were obliged to go away without the bread of life for which they came.

"The Academy of Music, the largest and most splendid audience-room in the United States, was then hired at great expense for the winter season, or as long as it should be required; and pastors of the various churches cordially agreed to give their services in preaching the gospel to the vast congregations gathered every Sabbath evening within those walls.

"But while these great movements command public mention in this history of these times of revival, it must not be forgotten that the chief instrument that God has employed is the faithful, constant, and earnest preaching of the word by pastors to their own flocks. I have reason to know that some of the most favoured churches have been those that are out of the great centres of attraction, in the retired and waste places of the city.

"Among the most efficient agencies to bring the truth directly to the hearts of men, in this and other cities, has been the wide circulation of brief, pungent, evangelical tracts, urging Christians to double diligence in the service of Christ, and warning the wicked to flee from the wrath to come. The societies having this as their special work, bear witness to the fact, that such tracts have been in demand to an extent unexampled before; and private benevolence and zeal have given still greater impetus to the same form of Christian effort.

"Another feature of the work is, that it has been conducted by laymen. It began with them; it continues with them. Clergymen share in the conduct, but no more than laymen. They are often seen in these assemblies, but they assume no control. They are in no way distinguishable from others. They oftener sit silent through the meeting than otherwise. Clergymen come to the place precisely for the same reason that others do—because it is the place of *prayer*. They say and feel as others say and feel—'It is good for me to draw near to God.'

"In all former revivals, a few, not the many, have done all the labour, and felt all the responsibility of the occasion. The minister would be weighed down under the burden of new cares which would come upon him. A few would be willing to share with him the labours of the work, but the great mass of Christians would stand still and see the salvation of God.

"In all former revivals, the hidden, aggregate power of a thoroughly-awakened laity was not known. In *this* it has been more developed and manifested than ever before; and even now is only beginning to be fully understood. GOD has been working in such a way as to shew more than ever the power, not of the ministry only, but of the *Church*. And He has done this in a way to arouse no unholy jealousies in any quarter. Never before, in these latter days, have ministers found such abundant help in the Church; never have they preached and laboured with such courage and hope. So far as this city was concerned, the organised systems of tract and Sunday-school visitation had much to do with the beginning of this revival, with its spread, and with its continuance to the present hour. The latter part of last year a more thorough system was resolved upon, of searching out and exploring the destitution of this great city, and inducing the *neglected* and *neglecting* thousands to attend upon the worship of God. It was determined to push this plan of visitation into the fashionable avenues as well as into the 'highways and hedges' of the city. The numbers were greatly increased of those who visited the '*house of prayer.*' All denominations nearly were benefited by this work, and many of them shared in the labour of it. In many Sunday-schools, the numbers were doubled, in all increased. In this way, thousands of persons—some from the 'brown stone fronts,' and some from the garrets and cellars—swelled the numbers, who were seen on Sunday morning wending their way to the sanctuary. 'High life and low life' were on the street together, and in the house of God together. This system of visitation was adopted and carried out in New York and Brooklyn about the same time. It was an organised plan adopted by the churches to visit in their respective localities, and search out every kind of destitution.

"Among the members of our churches, there has been a sad want of a sense of individual obligation, and proper appreciation of the value of personal effort. The present revival has wrought a revolution in men's minds in this respect. A power has been developed which was almost unknown to the modern church. It was the power of personal fidelity to souls; the power of individual, personal effort for their salvation; the power of prayer and effort when concentrated upon one specific object; the power of love, when an individual feels that it follows him with unceasing anxiety and importunity, and never despairs of its object till it is securely housed in the ark of safety.

"'Go ye into all the world, and preach the gospel to every creature,' has commonly been regarded as the great commission to the *preachers* of the gospel. Now it was felt to be a commission which is given to every Christian, that we are bound to carry the gospel message to every individual mind and heart—'every creature' in highways and byways, in garrets and cellars, in parlours and counting-rooms, in cottages and palaces, wherever there is a 'creature' who is impenitent, to him, to her, we are to 'preach the gospel.' We are to preach it as the great remedy for the woes of the perishing world. Every one is to preach it to every one, till there is no need of preaching it, 'for all shall know the Lord from the least to the greatest.'

"In this revival, men have been astonished at the success with which they can 'preach the gospel.' They have been astonished at the efficacy of lay labour and individual effort. Impenitent men have been found ready to hear, and ready to obey the gospel call. This very discovery has roused up the individual faithfulness of Christians, and they have felt the value of personal effort, as they never felt it before since the days of the first Christians. Men have been surprised at the success of a little labour; and this has encouraged more labour. It is felt, too, that the Christian must preach and keep preaching; that he must take hold of the sinner, and never let go till he is brought into the kingdom of Christ. Not that *he* can bring him in, but God can bring him in through the faithful believer's instrumentality.

"It was often made the subject of prayer, that none who came there to pray might go away to do business according to what were commonly denominated the 'laws of trade.' We remember that men of business prayed that they might always be enabled to do business on Christian principles, and go from the prayer-meeting to carry out the principles of the gospel into daily life. There has been a great quickening of the consciences of men in regard to this matter. Much that was done in business was considered to be in direct contravention of the laws of Christ's house. Many have had great trials in their own minds in regard to their business. Some have felt that they must give up their pursuits, or lose their souls. Thus the power of the revival is felt in all departments of business, and controls the public commercial conscience, compelling men to do right. We believe, that for integrity and uprightness, no men stand higher than the merchants of New York. But we must admit, in all candour, that here was a field where the power of this revival was intensely needed. There never was that high tone of honour which could not be a higher tone. The length and breadth of a man's honour should not be measured by his punctuality in paying his notes, while a thousand impositions and abuses crept into his mode of doing business, some of which he might *know*. Hundreds of men in this city and in other cities have long been in the habit of suffering things to be done in their name, under the false assumption of necessity, that would never bear the light of eternity, and that would be condemned by every conscience enlightened by the Word of God. When these white frauds, these little deceptions, these concealments of truth, no better than declarations of the false, were exposed in the light of the prayer-meeting, a discovery was made that startled hundreds from their self-confident security, and led them to repentance. It was admitted, and it was felt that doing business on Christian principles meant to arrest these evils—meant to uphold the standard so high, that even the most rigid interpretation of the gospel would not condemn it.

"What has been the effect of the revival in this regard? It has had a powerful influence in the direction of correcting abuses all over the land. It has sunk down deep into the consciences of men, and instructed them in their duty. It has shed its light upon the hearts of men in all branches of trade, and made them feel what the laws of the gospel demand in all the business relations of life."

May God bless and prosper that people, among whom the Christian virtues are so extensively cultivated, and upon whom He has so largely poured out of His Spirit! May He enable them to suppress the rebellion; and then to serve Him in peace and in prosperity better than they have ever done!

CHAPTER II.

ON SLAVERY IN THE SLAVE STATES.

ELEVEN States have seceded from the American Union. The first seven were—South Carolina, Mississippi, Alabama, Florida, Georgia, Louisiana, and Texas. Then followed—Virginia, Arkansas, Tennessee, and North Carolina. They have an aggregate area of 733,645 square miles, and their population is as follows:—

States.	Whites and Free.	Slaves.	Total.
Alabama,	529,164	435,132	964,296
Arkansas,	324,323	111,104	435,427
Florida,	78,686	61,753	140,439
Georgia,	595,097	462,230	1,057,327
Louisiana,	376,913	332,520	709,433
Mississippi,	354,699	436,696	791,395
N. Carolina,	661,586	331,081	992,667
S. Carolina,	301,271	402,541	703,812
Texas,	420,651	180,388	601,039
Tennessee,	834,063	275,784	1,109,847
Virginia,	1,105,196	490,887	1,596,083
Total,	5,581,649	3,520,116	9,101,765
Total in all Slave States,	8,280,490	3,949,557	12,230,047

In these States the slave system, which is nearly the same in all, may be briefly described in the following particulars:—

1. The slave-holder has the legal right to buy and sell men, women, and children.

2. He has the legal right to work them without wages under the whip.

3. His legal power over them is nearly absolute.

4. Without the violation of any State law, he may treat them with much cruelty, because they have no legal rights.

5. Without the violation of any State law, he may corrupt as much as he pleases their wives and daughters, because, according to law, they have no conjugal rights.

6. Whatever the law may be, he may, in contempt of law, commit almost any crime against them with impunity, because they may not complain against him to any magistrate, nor give evidence against him in any court of justice.

7. He may keep them in any degree of ignorance, because the law forbids any one to teach them to read, and allows him to flog them if they go off the estate without his leave, even to attend public worship.

This system, as it exists in law and practice, I will briefly examine, that we may see how far the slave-holders are entitled to our sympathy for having rebelled against their government and their country, that they might uphold and perpetuate it.

SECTION I.—THE HOME SLAVE TRADE.

In all the Slave States, slaves can be bought and sold; and from any one of these States slaves can be

exported into other States and sold as merchandise.*
Children above five years old are sold with or without
their parents, and parents with or without their children. Husbands are sold without their wives, and
wives without their husbands. Brothers and sisters
are separated by sale, and young girls are sold alone
to any one who chooses to buy them.

Various causes occasion their sale. They are sold
because the owner has fallen into debt, or because he
wants money, or because the owner has so directed in
his will, or because his executor must divide his property among his heirs. Some are sold from spite, and
some because they prove intractable; but in the Border
States they are sold by the gentlemen who breed them
as a regular source of income.

They may be sold by private contract or by public
auction to planters or to traders. These again sell
them privately, or expose them publicly to sale in
their pens. In all the Slave States there is a considerable sale of men and women, some owners wishing to
sell and others to buy; but the sales are chiefly effected
in the Border States, because, these being overstocked,
the proprietors turn their surplus stock into money.
The Virginian breeders alone sell men and women
annually to the amount of eight millions of dollars,
which at eight hundred dollars for each slave would
equal ten thousand sales.† From the sale of these
men and women of the working-classes, the gentlemen

---

* The Secession War, by Colonel Shaffner, 292.
† Patton, 25.

derive a large part of their wealth. "The first families of Virginia live on slave-breeding. The annual sale of slaves from that State amounts to eight millions of dollars. This will account for the intense zeal of a faction to carry that State out of the Union in opposition to the strong popular vote to the contrary." *

"In the States of Maryland, Virginia, North Carolina, Kentucky, Tennessee, and Missouri, as much attention is paid to the breeding and growth of negroes as to that of horses and mules. Planters command their girls and women, married or unmarried, to have children. I have known a great many girls to be sold off because they did not have children." "The number of slaves exported to the Cotton States is considerably more than twenty thousand a-year."

"Mr Ellison gives the annual importations, for the ten years ending 1860, into seven of the Southern States, from the slave-trading States, as 26,301."†

The sale of a child by a slave-owner involves a double robbery:—First, from the parents, to whom God has given their child to be trained up in His fear, (Ps. cxxvii. 3, 4; Eph. vi. 4,)—the slave-holder having no more right to take their child than they have to take his. If he might accuse them of robbery for selling his child, they may accuse him of robbery for selling theirs. Secondly, he robs the child of his liberty. As a negro would commit a robbery if he were to seize some slave-holders and sell them, because their limbs and their minds are their own; so a slave-holder is

* Ibid., 25, 20. † Olmsted, i. 58.

guilty of a similar robbery when he sells negroes. What more right has he to his limbs than they have to theirs? God has given them liberty as one of their inalienable rights, and no human law, no custom, no legal instrument can make the sale cease to be a robbery. Every successive purchase is a new robbery. The transfer of stolen property from one thief to another cannot communicate any right over the property to the second. If a thief steals my purse, and sells it to another thief, the second has no more right to it than the first. As the first had no right to sell, so the second had no right to buy what belongs to me. Slaveholders, then, are guilty of holding wrongfully what is the inalienable property of another, and, whether buyers or sellers, are simply men-stealers.

Among many instances of these sales, I will cite one or two:—"The public sale of slaves in the market-place at Charleston occurs frequently. I was present at two sales, when, especially at one of them, the miserable creatures were in tears on account of their being separated from their relations and friends. At one of them, a young woman of sixteen or seventeen was separated from her father and mother, all her relations, and every one she had formerly known." *

"Curiosity sometimes leads me to auction sales of the negroes. A few days since, I attended one which exhibited the beauties of slavery. There I saw the father looking sullen contempt on the crowd, and expressing an indignation in his countenance that he dared not

* Stuart, ii. 110.

speak, and the mother pressing her infants closer to her bosom, and exclaiming, while the tears chased down her cheeks, 'I can't leff my children, I won't leff my children;' but on the hammer went. On another stand, I saw a man apparently as white as myself exposed for sale. At another time, I saw the concluding scene of this infernal drama: a slave-ship for New Orleans was lying in the stream, and the negroes, hand-cuffed and pinioned, were hurried off in boats, eight at a time. Here I witnessed the last farewell, the mute and agonising embrace of husband and wife. It was a living death. They never see or hear of each other any more. Tears flowed fast, and mine with the rest."*

"On one of these sale days, I saw a mother lead seven children to the auction block: she knew that some of them would be taken from her, but they took all. The children were sold to a slave-trader, and their mother was bought by a man in her own town. I met their mother in the street, and her wild haggard face lives in my mind. She wrung her hands in anguish, and exclaimed, 'Gone—all gone—why don't God kill me!'"†

"There were three young negroes outside the cabin. They were boys; the oldest twelve or fourteen years old, the youngest not more than seven; they had evidently been bought lately by their present owner, and probably had just been taken from their parents. They

---

* Letter from Charleston, in Stuart, ii. 110.
† The Deeper Wrong, 27.

lay on the deck and slept, with no bed and no cover but a single blanket for each. The older ones were continually teasing the younger, who seemed very sad. He would get very angry, and sometimes strike them. He would then be driven into a corner, where he would lie on his back and kick at them, in a perfect frenzy of anger and grief. Once, when they had plagued him in this way for some time, he jumped up to the cotton bales, and made as if he would have plunged overboard. One of the older boys caught him by the ankle, and held him till his master came and gave him a severe flogging. A number of passengers collected about them, and I heard several say, 'That's what he wants.' Red River said to me, 'He's got the devil in him right bad; and he 'll hev to take a right many of them warmings before it will be got out.'"* Poor child! torn from his parents at the age of seven, sleeping at night without a bed, tormented, driven to desperation by his misery, then flogged for being miserable, and without a single friend to utter one word of kindness to him in his despair!

"When I left Mr R——'s, I was driven about twenty miles by one of his house-servants. After a silence of some minutes, he said abruptly, 'If I was free I would go to Virginia, and see my old mudder. I don't well know exactly how old I is; but I rec'lect de day I was taken away from my ole mudder, she tell me I was tirteen year old.' He did not like to come away at all: he felt dreadful bad. He was

* Olmsted, i. 280.

brought with a great many other negroes in waggons to Louisville; and then they were put on board a steamboat, and brought down here."*

The following was a scene in the slave market at Richmond:—"The woman, with three children, was neatly attired. Her children were all girls, one of them a baby at the breast three months old, and the others two and three years of age respectively. 'Are you a married woman?' 'Yes, sir.' 'How many children have you had?' 'Seven.' 'Where is your husband?' 'In Madison county.' 'When did you part with him?' 'On Wednesday, two days ago.' 'Were you sorry to part from him?' 'Yes, sir; my heart was a'most broke.' 'Why is your master selling you?' 'I don't know; he wants money to buy some land; suppose he sells me for that.' 'Sale is going to commence! this way, gentlemen!' cried a man at the door to a number of loungers outside; and all having assembled, the mulatto assistant led the woman and her children to the block. There she stood with her infant at the breast, and one of her girls on each side. 'Well, gentlemen,' began the salesman, 'here is a capital woman and her three children, all in good health; what do you say for them? Give me an offer. I put up the whole lot at 850 dollars: will no one advance upon that? A fine healthy baby—hold it up— (mulatto takes the baby from the woman's breast and holds it aloft)—that will do. A woman still young, and three children, all for 850 dollars! An advance,

* Ibid., i. 333.

if you please, gentlemen. (860.) Thank you for 860. Any one bids more?' (870. And so on the bidding goes as far as 890 dollars, when it stops.) 'That won't do, gentlemen. I cannot take such a low price. She may go down.'"*

"A slave stood on the auction-block in the town of L——. After displaying the athletic form of the chattel, the auctioneer eulogised him thus:—'Him's a nigger as good as you could see, rising twenty-eight, sound as an oak, honest, industrious, sober, hain't the mark of a lash upon him. (1000 dollars.) You could trust him with your wife and your children, your keys and your money. (1100, 1200.) He was converted four years ago; he's as good as a preacher among yer cattle. (1250, 1300, 1400.) He's got the Holy Spirit; he can pray, and sing, and preach; he keeps all the commandments; he can preach like the bishop himself.' After a spirited competition, the Christian slave, the elder of a Southern church, was knocked down for 1850 dollars."†

"A gentleman told me that, as he was passing through Virginia this winter, a man entered the car in which he was seated, leading in a negro girl, whose manner and expression of face indicated dread and grief. Thinking she was a criminal, he asked the man what she had done. 'Done? Nothing.' 'What are you going to do with her?' 'I'm taking her down to Richmond to be sold.' 'Does she belong to you?' 'No; she belongs to ——; he raised her.'

* Olmsted, ii. 375. † Aspects of Religion, &c., 115.

'Why does he sell her? Has she done anything wrong?' 'No; she's no fault, I reckon.' 'Then what does he want to sell her for?' 'Sell her for? Why shouldn't he sell her? He sells one or more every year; wants the money for 'em, I reckon.' The irritated tone and severe stare with which this was said, my friend took as a caution not to pursue the investigation."*

"Antoinette, the flower of the family, a girl who was much beloved by all who knew her, for her Christ-like piety, as well as her great talents and extreme beauty, was bought by an uneducated and drunken slave-dealer. The trader said to a kind lady who wished to purchase Antoinette out of his hands, 'I reckon I'll not sell the smart critter for 10,000 dollars. I always wanted her for my own use.' 'You should remember, sir, that there is a just God.' 'I does; and guess it's monstrous kind in Him to send such likely niggers for our convenience.' Antoinette became frantic. I can never forget her cries of despair when Horkins gave the order for her to be taken to his house, and locked in an upper room. On his entering the apartment, a fearful struggle ensued. Antoinette broke from him, pitched herself head-foremost from the window, and fell upon the pavement below. Her bruised body was soon picked up; her spirit had fled. Horkins drank more than ever; and, in a short time, he died raving mad, with delirium tremens."†

These dealers are the great agents in the home slave-trade; they are thus described by Colonel Shaffner:—

* Olmsted, i. 58. † Running a Thousand Miles, 23.

"A slave-trader in Virginia purchases ten, twenty, or more men, women, and children; and when he has got a sufficient number, he takes them to a more Southern market. They are well clad and fed. The children ride in the waggon, the women walk separately, and the men are chained together. Thus fastened and shackled, they march behind the waggon. The owner rides on his horse behind his slave-gang, well armed."*

In Virginia, the slaves are drawn off almost as fast as they grow up, to grow cotton in the more Southern States.† "Labourers," says Mr Olmsted, "are being constantly sent away; I have not been on or seen a railroad train departing southward, that did not convey a considerable number of the best class of negro labourers, in charge of a trader, who was intending to sell them to cotton planters."‡ The slave population, once greater than that of the whites, has been reduced by emigration and sale, till there are now less than half as many slaves as whites.§

The number exported to the Cotton States from the Border States is more than twenty thousand a-year.∥ Of this trade, John Randolph, himself a slave-holder, said on the floor of Congress, "What are the trophies of this infernal traffic? The handcuff, the manacles, the bloodstained cowhide."¶ Even Mr Spratt, who strongly advocates the re-opening of the African slave-trade, seems to doubt whether this home trade is not inhuman, for he there speaks of slaves to be transferred

---

* Shaffner, 292.   † Olmsted, i. 113.   ‡ Ibid., 112.
§ Ibid., 115.   ∥ Ibid., 58.   ¶ Ibid., 356.

from a Border State to the Mississippi:—"These must have been well raised, and have become attached to a home. They must have relatives and friends, or wives and husbands. They must leave a life to which they have been accustomed, and a land particularly favoured, for one not more favoured in the West; and it is doubted whether such a change of condition, such a rupture of ties, such an abandonment of all that is dear and familiar, from no motive of their own, but from the interest of some other person in no way related to them, is not the sadder object of the two."* Mr Spratt then thinks that the Virginian slave trade is more cruel than the African, and yet from that home trade the gentlemen of Virginia gain their wealth.

SECTION II.—SLAVE LABOUR.

The labourers upon the estate of a cotton planter in one of the Slave States are his machines for moneymaking, from which he has to obtain wealth by compelling them to raise for him as much cotton as they can. Of course he does not give them wages for their labour any more than he would to a machine. From self-interest he keeps them in tolerable working order, as he would clean and grease the wheels of his mill: but he does nothing more; because all which he might expend upon them, beyond bare necessaries, would be taken from his income. He therefore feeds them on the coarsest fare, such as Indian corn and beans, with a little bacon. Their clothing is the cheapest he can

* Spratt, *Star*, Sept. 2, 1862.

procure, coarse cotton shirts and trousers, the women receiving similar materials; and their houses for the most part are log huts, which he does not furnish, and which, without time or money, they cannot furnish for themselves.

Mr Spratt writes, "Each slave can be fed and clothed for less than 25 dollars per annum. Twenty-five dollars will be all the cost of his employment."* And as the wages of a labourer at the North are a dollar a-day, the planters who maintain them at the cost allowed by Mr Spratt, instead of giving them each half a dollar a-day, which is half the wages of a labourer in New England, and less than they would get under a system of free labour, these rob each of them of 131 dollars annually.

According to Mr Olmsted, the negro's loss is less: but we must recollect that he describes his actual loss according to the price of labour under the slave system. The wages paid to an owner for an able-bodied slave are 120 dollars per annum; and the cost of his maintenance being 30 dollars, the remainder, 90 dollars, is stolen from him.† On the lowest calculation, therefore, the slave-holders enrich themselves by cheating each of their labourers annually out of 90 dollars.

The owner having thus arranged to maintain his slaves in the cheapest manner possible, has now to obtain from them the greatest possible returns. The hours of their field labour vary in different States and

---

* *Star*, August 28. † Olmsted, i. 117; ii. 230, 237.

at different times of the year, from eleven hours to fifteen; and on some estates during crop they run to eighteen. Nothing can get it out of their heads that all this labour is extorted from them by injustice; although preachers and planters assure them that God made them for their masters, they still think that He made them for themselves. And when they see that their masters obtain wealth, splendour, ease, and power through their toils, they will obstinately conclude that a large part of their gains have been stolen from them.

Almost universally men shrink from profitless labours; and, therefore, when negroes seek to avoid toils, of which their masters reap all the profits, they only therein resemble other men. What inducements have they to be industrious? Assiduity brings them neither money, nor clothes, nor food, nor even thanks. Why, then, should they work hard? When planters generally say that negroes are lazy, they only express the fact that like all other men they wish to keep as much of their own as they can, from the robber who is too strong for them.

But, whatever may be its origin, this general indisposition in them to labour for their masters must be overcome by some motive, or these planters would be ruined. Rewards for industry, strict justice, opportunities for self-improvement, occasional rest, and, above all, real kindness, would, even in their state of slavery, make them zealous in their work; but a coarse, selfish, imperious nature is incapable of using these methods;

which are, indeed, so exceptional as to be almost unknown. The planters, therefore, resort to the whip, which everywhere takes the place of wages.

Roused to their work at sunrise by the horn of the driver, they work twelve hours daily under his whip, doing as little as they can, that they may reserve for themselves some of that strength the whole of which is properly their own. To exhaust themselves as little as possible is to obtain from him who has robbed them a small part of their right. To be as listless and indifferent over their work as a beast would be is natural, for since their owner treats them as beasts, they may justly give him nothing but a bestial service. This system creates much misery. What would our feelings be if we found ourselves reduced to work twelve hours a-day without wages, and without the hope of mending our condition, from January to December? With what zeal could we do this for a selfish tyrant, continually revolving in his mind how he could lessen the sums which he must spend upon our maintenance, and how he might extort more work out of our weariness? By this system the master degrades his labourers. God made them to develop their powers; to observe, inquire, converse, read, and think; to cultivate their mechanical skill, to multiply their comforts, to educate their children; and their master, shutting them out from their prerogative of men, condemns them to labour as beasts, without thought, without aim, without hope, receiving in return, like beasts, a feed of corn at night, and permission to lie down in the straw.

Several other evil consequences follow from this robbery on the one side and the resentment of it on the other. For as the wealth of the master has been stolen from the men, to get back a part of it seems to them a species of justice. Even decent and thoughtful negroes sometimes steal from their masters when they would not steal from any one else. But stealing leads to lying, for if a man steals he must lie to avoid detection. Nor is this the only cause of lying. All sorts of lies have in fact become common among the slaves. They lie to avoid work, to prevent punishment, to obtain a favour, to secure a method of escape. Lying is the easiest defence of the oppressed against the oppressor; and slaves must be strongly tempted to it, when speaking the truth would increase their burdens or their sufferings. Thus in the condition of the slave right and wrong become confounded, and they are demoralised by a system which allows them no right except those which they can obtain by theft and conceal by falsehood. Idleness, theft, and lying are three vices, which, as long as it lasts, slavery must inevitably generate; and the slave-holder should cease to ascribe to their special depravity what is mainly the effect of his own injustice.

I will now subjoin a few testimonies which confirm and illustrate the foregoing sketch.

The following is Mr Olmsted's account of an estate upon a tributary of the Mississippi:—

"The property consisted of four plantations, each with its own negro cabins and overseer, all under a manager. These five men, each living more than a mile from either of the others, were the only white men on the estate, and the only others within several miles of them were a few skulking vagabonds. As the testimony of negroes against them would not be received as evidence in court, there was very little probability that any excessive severity would be restrained by fear of the law.

"Each overseer regulated the hours of work on his own plantation. I saw the negroes at work before sunrise and after sunset. The ploughs at work, both with single and double mule teams, were generally held by women. They were superintended by a negro man, who carried a whip, which he frequently cracked at them. They are constantly driven up to their work, and the stupid, plodding, machine-like manner in which they labour is painful to witness. This was especially the case with the hoe gangs. I repeatedly rode through the lines at a canter with other horsemen, often coming upon them suddenly without producing the smallest change in the dogged action of the labourers, or causing one of them, so far as I could see, to lift an eye from the ground. A powerful negro walked to and fro in the rear of the line, frequently cracking his whip, and calling out in the surliest manner, 'Shove your hoe there! Shove your hoe.'"*

Another estate is thus described:—"We were passing a large old plantation, the cabins of the negroes upon which were wretched hovels, small, without win-

* Olmsted, ii. 201, 202.

dows, and dilapidated. A large gang of negroes were at work, planting cane. Two white men were sitting on horseback looking at them, and a negro-driver was walking among them, with a whip in his hand. The slaves appeared to be working hard: they were shabbily clothed, had a cowed expression, looking on the ground, not even glancing at us as we passed, and were perfectly silent." *

Mr Stuart was not much impressed with the kindness shewn to domestic slaves. "I made," he says, in South Carolina, "a stop on my way at a pretty large plantation where guests were admitted. The slaves were numerous, and were, I had reason to believe, from what I afterwards learned, as well treated as they generally are in this country; but it did not seem to me that their want of education, and the want of ordinary comforts, place them in a situation much removed from the brutes. They had little clothing, all of one drab colour; and not one of them had bed-clothes. Every one of them with whom I had an opportunity of conversing declared themselves unhappy and miserable. A certain task is allotted to each of them, and if this is not done, they are subjected to one of three punishments—whipping, wearing irons, or putting in the stocks." †

In Louisiana the law requires that every owner shall give his slaves one barrel of Indian corn, or the equivalent thereof in rice, beans, or other grain, every month. ‡ "They have three meals per day; for

* Olmsted, I. 340. † Stuart, ii. 83, 84. ‡ Shaffner, 288.

breakfast and supper they have coffee, bread, and meat, and at dinner they have vegetables, meat, bread," &c.* Colonel Shaffner is a friend of the slave-holders, and records probably some very favourable instances which he has known. Mr Olmsted, who travelled widely, says, " I have no doubt that suffering from want of food is rare. The food is everywhere however coarse, crude, and wanting in variety; much more so than that of our prison convicts." † "I was told in Virginia that I should find them better fed in Louisiana than anywhere else." "Ninety-nine in a hundred of our free labourers live, in respect of food, at least four times as well as the average of the harder-worked slaves in the Louisiana sugar plantations." ‡

Colonel Shaffner reports, "They are well clad and fed. Their clothes are of plain woollen or cotton materials, and they are provided with shoes, hats, stockings, and bed-clothes." § Mr Olmsted agrees with Colonel Shaffner on this point, except that the bed-clothes dwindle down to "one blanket." And he adds instances like the following :—"After midnight, as we were retiring to our rooms, our progress up-stairs and along the corridors was several times impeded by negroes lying fast asleep in their usual clothes only, upon the floor. I asked why they were not in bed, and was answered by a gentleman, that negroes never wanted to go to bed; they always preferred to sleep on the floor." ‖

* Shaffner, 239. † Olmsted, ii. 241. ‡ Ibid., 239.
§ Shaffner, 239. ‖ Olmsted, i. 105.

"Beyond the excessive labour required of them on some plantations," a planter said, "he did not think slaves were often treated with unnecessary cruelty. It was necessary to use the lash occasionally. Slaves never felt under any moral obligation to obey their masters. They were obedient just so far as they saw that they must be to avoid punishment."[*]

"It is told me as a singular fact, that everywhere on the plantations the agrarian notion has become a fixed point of the negro system of ethics: that the result of labour belongs of right to the labourer; and on this ground, even the religious feel justified in using massa's property for their own benefit. This they term taking, and it is never admitted to be a reproach to a man among them that he is charged with it; though stealing or taking from another than their master is so."[†]

Jefferson says, "That disposition to theft with which they have been branded must be ascribed to their situation, and not to any depravity of the moral sense. The man in whose favour no laws of property exist, feels himself less bound to respect those made in favour of others." "It is a problem which I give to the master to solve, whether the religious precepts against the violation of property were not planned for him as well as his slave; and whether the slave may not justifiably take a little from one who has taken all from him."[‡]

[*] Olmsted, ii. 101.   [†] Ibid., i. 106.   [‡] Ibid.

SECTION III.—THE POWER OF THE SLAVE-HOLDER.

The negroes are the working-classes from whose labours the slave-holders obtain wealth, splendour, ease, and power. It is therefore essential to the governing class that they should be able to secure their labours. The master is the sole judge of the amount of service which his slaves must render; and this service he must have power to secure from each, because, if one could refuse to render it, all the others might. Those negroes are the most reluctant to obey their owner who have most intellect and most spirit, their intellect revealing to them his injustice, and their spirit prompting them to resent it. A man with sense and spirit like Mr Craft must have feelings like his:—" The idea that we were held as chattels, and deprived of all legal rights; the thought that we had to give up our hard earnings to a tyrant, to enable him to live in idleness; the thought that we could not call the bones and sinews which God gave us our own; above all, the fact that another man had the power to tear from our cradle the new-born babe, sell it like a brute, and then scourge us if we dared to lift a finger to save it, haunted us for years."*

" Hundreds of slaves in New Orleans must be constantly reflecting, 'I am as capable of taking care of myself as this Irish hod-carrier, or this German market-gardener; why can't I have the enjoyment of my labour as well as they? I am as capable of taking care of my

* Craft, 1.

own family as they of theirs; why should I be subject to have them taken from me by those other men who call themselves our owners? I helped to build the school-house, and have not been paid for it. One thing I know, if they won't give me wages, I can take them.'"*

If such negroes could claim exemption from any service, all the rest would soon claim it. Hence a master must have the power of controlling the most enlightened, high-spirited, energetic, and brave, no less than the weaker; and the power requisite to control them must be very great. That power the law has put into his hands. He may work them without wages from sunrise to sunset all the year round, excepting Sundays.† He may flog them for passing the bounds of his estate to visit a neighbour,‡ or for going to public worship;§ he may take from them their property and their children;|| and he may sell them away from their wives, or their wives away from them.¶

"A slave is one who is in the power of a master to whom he belongs. The master may sell him, dispose of his person, his industry, and his labour. He can do nothing, possess nothing, nor acquire anything but what must belong to his master."**

"Slaves shall be deemed, taken, reputed, and judged in law to be chattels personal in the hands of their owners, to all intents, constructions, and purposes

---

* Olmsted, i. 300.   † Shaffner, 290.   ‡ Ibid., 285, 286.
§ Ibid., 280. || Ibid., 299, 294.   ¶ Ibid., 292, 294.
** Law of Louisiana; Craft, 17.

whatsoever." * "They are *things*, and are under the laws governing personal property with but a few limited exceptions." "The slave is considered a chattel."†

As a master may sell them at his pleasure, so if they forcibly resist his will, he may kill them. Colonel Shaffner gives indeed a hesitating denial of this fact, when he says, "The owner may advertise for his slave dead or alive; but woe be to the man who takes the life of a slave!" *The fugitive, however, cannot resist his arrest.*‡ What, then, if he does resist? Why, he will be shot. Mr Olmsted narrates many instances, and the law of Georgia is express:—"Any person who shall *maliciously* deprive a slave of his life shall suffer such punishment, &c., *except in case of insurrection by such slave*, and unless such death should happen by accident in giving such slave moderate correction."§ When, therefore, the slave resists, he may be deprived of life. "I have known slaves to be beaten to death; but as they died under 'moderate correction,' it was lawful, and, of course, the murderers were not interfered with."‖ Here is another law:—"If any slave who shall be out of the house or plantation where such slave shall live, shall refuse to submit to undergo the examination of any white person, it shall be lawful for such white person to pursue, apprehend,

---

* Brevard's Digest, 229; Craft, 17.   † Shaffner, 294, 296.
‡ Ibid., 290.   § Constitution of Georgia, art. iv., sec. 12; Craft, 17.
‖ Craft, 18.

and moderately correct such slave; *and if such slave shall assault and strike such white person, such slave may be lawfully killed."* *

"The cool way in which you hear the hanging of niggers, the shooting of niggers, talked of in bar-rooms, speaks volumes as to the exact state of the case. A negro was shot when running away near Greensborough, the day before I passed through, by a man who received instructions from the owner to take him alive, and shoot him if he resisted. I heard this discussed in the bar. One of the group summed up the arguments on both sides by exclaiming, 'Well, this shooting of niggers should be put a stop to; that's a fact.'" †

According to law, indeed, the master may not starve, mutilate, or *maliciously* kill his labourers; but the law is rendered nugatory by these three facts:—No negroes may give evidence against their master; if he is prudent, he will take care that no white men can; and if any white men could, they would not. The whole result is that the master has absolute power over his labourers. He can order any kind or amount of service, can enforce his orders by any means which he pleases, can flog, starve, and torture them as much and as often as he will, and in case of their forcible resistance, can kill them on the spot.

If they could have any legal rights, they would interfere with his power. They have therefore none. "Black

---

* Brevard's Digest, 231; Craft, 18.   † Olmsted, ii. 190.

men, says Chief-Justice Taney, have no rights which white men are bound to respect." * If this dictum be questionable with respect to negroes in the Free States, it is unquestionably true of slaves in the Slave States. How can chattels have rights? As slave-holders work them like beasts under the whip, they must deprive them of the rights of men.

It is essential to the system that all slave-holders alike should have this power, because the law can make no discrimination. Were all slave-holders just and benevolent, this power even in their hands would be oppressive and iniquitous; but unhappily the majority of our race are not benevolent and just. Slavery, too, begets in slave-holders many vices. Every one can see at once that the exercise of absolute power tends to make them selfish, imperious, irritable, harsh, and revengeful. They are selfish, because they think that the working-classes have been made for them; they are imperious, because every command of theirs, however unreasonable, must be instantly obeyed; they are irritable, because they are always suspecting that their commands will be opposed or evaded; they are harsh, because they find in their labourers many provoking faults; and they are revengeful, because their anger at the faults of a negro are increased by their contempt and their fear. Most reasonable were the following conclusions of Mr Jefferson:—"There must doubtless be an unhappy influence upon the manners of our people by the existence of slavery among us. The

* Patton, 20.

whole commerce between master and slave is a perpetual exercise of the most boisterous passions,—the most unremitting despotism on the one part, and degrading submission on the other. The man must be a prodigy who can retain his manners and morals undepraved by such circumstances."* But in every large class of men there are some worse than others. If, then, a slave-holder be ungodly, profligate, and cruel, if he be a brute and a savage, still he possesses all this legal power over his slaves; and who can tell what a terrible engine of oppression it must be in such hands? Who can say to what insults, wrongs, and outrages it must expose any of his slaves who are the objects of his wrath? There is nothing between them and death. Any one of them may die by inches, without any other white knowing anything about it. Whipping, imprisonment, starvation, and any other modes of torture which a hellish imagination can devise, may all be employed day by day to inflict misery upon the object of his hatred, without any interference of law, without any possibility even of complaint.

Such a power in the hands of selfish men seeking to extort wealth from their reluctant labourers would soon reduce the noblest race on earth to degradation. Any men treated as beasts must soon become stupid, improvident, idle, thoughtless, lying, pilfering, and sensual. Stupid, because all culture of mind is precluded; improvident, because their fodder is provided

* Helper, 153.

for them daily as for cattle, and they can hope for nothing more; idle, because they labour for an enemy, and can gain nothing by their industry; dishonest, because so only can they get back from their tyrant a small part of what he has stolen from them; lying, because by lies alone can they conceal their thefts or lighten their burdens; and sensual, because all mental, moral, and spiritual recreations are denied them.

Bought, sold, worked and whipped like beasts, accounted beasts by law, and thought by their owners to be beasts, it would be a miracle if they did not become bestial in their habits.

But under bad masters their degradation must be more rapid and complete. An ungodly man hates in others that godliness which thwarts him, and loves to see others as ungodly as himself. How then can the labourers of an ungodly planter serve God? He can forbid them to attend public worship; flog them if they meet to pray; and if any of them do pray, he can insult them as hypocrites, impose on them double tasks, and torment them with incessant punishments for presuming to be better than himself. Under a vicious planter how can slaves be virtuous, when his example, his patronage, his favours are all on the side of vice? When the demigod, whose property they are, is an adulterer, obscene in his conversation, and lawless in his life, a swearing, roaring, revelling, raging debauchee, how can his chattels be virtuous?

Indeed, it is too easy to see that under this system a bad man may compel his slaves to commit any crime whatsoever. If the God in heaven orders one thing, and the god on earth orders another, with the whip and the handcuff to back him, he must generally prevail. If he bids them lie, or steal, or torture a fellow-slave, or murder a neighbour, how can they oppose his terrible will when their opposition may expose them to be flogged, or starved, or kept in irons, or tortured even to death? When a planter keeps bloodhounds to hunt down fugitives, they will at his bidding tear a fugitive to pieces; and when he has reduced his labourers to be as submissive as dogs, he may make them, like his dogs, to accomplish any deed of blood. A black minister who had been pastor to negro churches in different parts of the Union, and who knew the Slave States well, said to me, "If you were to visit a plantation without a pass, and were thought to be an Abolitionist, a New Englander, or even an Englishman, the slaves, at the simplest sign from the planter, would tear you to pieces. The law has given him the power to exact from them any service which he pleases. And, as he has become their god, any order of his by which he means to gratify his lust, his cupidity, or his revenge, becomes to them like the law of God. Evil, which is his delight, becomes their duty; and at the bidding of an almighty fiend, they must prepare by the practice of every vice for an eternal hell, if they would not by their virtuous resistance to him turn the plantation on which they live into their hell on earth.

SECTION IV.—PROFLIGACY IN THE SLAVE STATES.

One inevitable result of slavery is a wide-spread profligacy pervading the community. The law of God is, that "every man should have his own wife," (1 Cor. vii. 2;) and Jesus has said of this relation, "*What God has joined together, let no man put asunder,*" (Matt. xix. 6.) But the slave-holders, assuming superiority to God, have ordered as follows:—"*The marriage between slaves is not a legal contract, and can be broken at the will of the owner. Their children are all illegitimate. They cannot be married by the law.*"* Of course, despite the tyranny of the slave-holders, two persons of the working-class can live together as man and wife; no law can hinder that; but "if the wife prove unfaithful, the husband cannot maintain an action against the adulterer. There are no remedies for adultery on either side."† A planter may seize and force the wife of a labourer without exposing himself to any legal penalty, the law allowing his deed, although Jesus has said, "*What God hath joined together, let no man put asunder.*" Slave-holders, in contempt of the law of God, continually separate them. "*The marriage is of no force in law. When in the midst of their happiness, surrounded by their children, their owner may . . . . sell them.*"‡ The law allows it. In fact, a working man's wife and daughter do not belong to him, but to the man who has bought them, to abuse or sell them as he will. Was there

* Shaffner, 294.   † Ibid., 295.   ‡ Ibid., 294.

ever before a society calling itself Christian, which so shamefully set aside the law of God to suit their own purposes? The effect of this upon the morals of the labourers is disastrous. "How is it possible to impress upon a negro the sacred obligation of marriage, by urging the precept not to put asunder what God has joined, while the laws of the country are teaching him an opposite lesson, by sending (at the caprice of his owner) himself to Maryland, his wife to Texas, and his children to Missouri, never to meet again?"[*] Mr Olmsted thus describes the state of things on one large and profitable estate:—"'Are those who are married true to each other?' The overseer laughed heartily, and described a disgusting state of things. Women were almost common property. 'Do you not try to discourage this?' 'No, not unless they quarrel.' 'You punish them for adultery?' 'No, we punish them for quarrelling. If they don't quarrel, I don't mind anything about it.'"[†] "One of the chief causes of the immorality of negroes arises from the indifference both of themselves and of their owners to family relations."[‡]

But there are other laws in the Slave States respecting marriage. No woman who is a slave can marry a free coloured man.[§] No woman who is a slave can marry a white man.[||] No woman who is black or

---

[*] Godley, ii. 215.   [†] Olmsted, ii. 200.
[‡] Testimony of an excellent Presbyterian minister; Olmsted, ii. 218.
[§] Linda Brent, 58.   [||] Craft, 20.

brown, even if she be free, can marry a white man.* Hence all intercourse between slave-holders and coloured women must be vicious. While thus marriage is discredited, and all the children of the working-classes are treated as illegitimate, those classes must become indifferent to family relations. Girls are thus taught by the laws of their country, and by the custom of society, to regard vicious and virtuous habits as equally good. They are from the beginning vitiated by all that they witness. Women who are taught by the law that they are chattels, not persons—things, not women — personal property, not accountable moral agents, are placed in the hands of owners or agents who may be remorseless libertines, without protection, without appeal to any judge for redress, without even the right of complaint. So placed, they are tempted, flattered, bribed, by planters, by their sons, by their managers, by their overseers, to degrade themselves; and if they do not listen to these offers, they can be soon tormented into compliance. "No pen can give an adequate description of the all-pervading corruption produced by slavery. The slave-girl is reared in an atmosphere of licentiousness and fear. The lash and the foul talk of her master and his sons are her teachers. When she is fourteen or fifteen, her owner, or his sons, or the overseer, or perhaps all of them, begin to bribe her with presents. If these fail to accomplish their purpose, she is whipped or starved into submission to their will." "Fathers, husbands, and

* Craft, 20.

brothers have no right to defend their daughters, wives, and sisters, and should they attempt it, may soon be made to repent of their temerity."* "When I had been in the family a few weeks, one of the plantation slaves was brought to town; Dr Flint ordered him to be taken to the workhouse, and tied up to the joist so that his feet would just escape the ground. I never shall forget that night. Never before in my life had I heard hundreds of blows fall upon a human being. His piteous groans, and his 'Oh, pray don't, massa!' rang in my ear for months afterwards. Some said master accused him of stealing corn; others said he had quarrelled with his wife in presence of the overseer, and had accused his master of being the father of her child—they were both black, and the child was very fair. A few months afterwards Dr Flint handed them both over to a slave-trader. When the mother was delivered into the trader's hands, she said, 'You promised to treat me well;' to which he replied, 'You have let your tongue run too far; damn you.'†

This is the condition, not of a few persons who have been reduced to slavery by their crimes, but of the working-classes of a large territory, who, having committed no offence, have as much right to liberty as their masters have. No class of men could be safely entrusted with this power; and least of all the slaveholders, who are proverbially impetuous, impulsive, self-willed, and, more than most men, likely to be the slaves of their own passions.

* Linda Brent, 79. † Ibid., 23.

This licentiousness in the Slave States prevails the more extensively because it contributes to the wealth of the slaveholders. Planters may make much more by selling their children, or their grandchildren, or any brown, than they can by the sale of pure blacks. While a healthy black girl may sell for 650 dollars, a handsome brown girl, the daughter or the granddaughter of a planter, may bring him 1200. No slave girls so replenish his purse as those who are light-coloured. Under these circumstances, profligacy must be very common. "We do not suppose," says Colonel Shaffner, "it would be possible for an owner of a slave that had a child by his own servant to be permitted to live in any community in the Southern States."* "It is a common practice," replies Mr Craft, "for gentlemen to be the fathers of children by their slaves, whom they can and do sell; and the more beautiful and virtuous the girls are, the greater the price they bring."† About one-fourth of all the slaves in Mississippi and Louisiana are browns.‡

The following is the testimony of Mr Stuart:—"Here (at Georgetown) we were joined by a very wealthy and well-known planter of South Carolina, and afterwards by a medical man. . . . . The planter and the doctor seemed to be on intimate terms. The doctor asked the planter what could have induced him to stay at a plantation during the unhealthy season. He said, he found that half a dozen of the girls could no longer be trusted without a husband, and that he

* Shaffner, 295.   † Craft, 20.   ‡ Olmsted, ii. 210.

thought it was not only for his interest but for the plantation generally that he should be the first husband; and the doctor, who gave us similar accounts of the management of his slaves, admitted the validity of the reason. In the course of the conversation which followed, it turned out that this planter was frequently waited upon at table by his own children, and had sent some of them to the public market to be sold as slaves."*

"Marriage among the slaves is allowed, but where a young man has a fine family, the planter very often, with a view to the increase of his stock, forces him to have many wives; and in the same way married females are often obliged to receive more husbands than one, as the planter may order. In fact, the slaves are as much obliged to obey the commands of their masters in respect to sexual intercourse as anything else."†

About one-fourth of all the slaves in Mississippi are browns.‡ In Virginia they are not much less numerous apparently, according to the following testimony of Mr Olmsted:—"I am surprised at the number of fine-looking mulattoes or nearly white coloured persons that I see. The majority of those with whom I have come personally in contact are such."§ "My master," says Linda Brent, "was to my knowledge the father of eleven slaves. But did the mothers dare to tell who was the father of their children? They knew too well

* Stuart, ii. 92-94.   † Ibid., 86.
‡ Olmsted, ii. 210.   § Ibid., i. 40.

the terrible consequences."* This is her account of another planter:—Three sisters were carried to their master's plantation. "The eldest soon became a mother; and when the slave-holder's wife looked at her babe she wept bitterly. She had a second child by her master, and then he sold her and her offspring to his brother. She bore two children to his brother, and was sold again. The next sister went crazy.; the life she was compelled to lead drove her mad." †

"I write only that whereof I know. I can testify from my own experience and observation that slavery is a curse to the whites as well as the blacks. It makes the white fathers cruel and sensual, the sons violent and licentious; it contaminates the daughters, and makes the wives wretched." ‡

Mrs Douglas, a Virginia woman, who was tried, convicted, and punished a year or two since for teaching a number of slaves to read, says in a letter from her jail: "The practice (amalgamation) is more general than the Southerners are willing to allow. Neither is it to be found only in the lower order of the white population. It pervades the entire society. Its followers are to be found among all ranks, occupations, and professions. The white mothers and daughters have suffered under it for years." §

"A large planter told, as a reason for sending his boys to be educated at the North, that there was no possibility of their being brought up in decency at

* Linda Brent, 55. † Ibid., 79.
‡ Ibid., 81. § Olmsted, i. 307.

home. Another planter told me that he was intending to move to a free country on this account. He said that the practice was not occasional or general; it was universal. There is not, he said, a likely-looking black girl in this State that is not the concubine of a white man. There is not an old plantation in which the grandchildren of the owner are not whipped in the field by his overseer." * Another Virginia proprietor told Mr Olmsted that he did not think that more than half the slaves there were full-blooded Africans.†

"Twice it happened to come to my knowledge that the sons of a planter, by whom I was lodged on this journey, lads of fourteen or sixteen, who were supposed to have slept in the same room with me, spent the night in the negro cabins." A Southern merchant visiting New York, said, "I have personal knowledge that there are but two lads sixteen years old in our town (a small market town of Alabama) who have not already had occasion to resort to remedies for the penalty of licentiousness."‡ In a letter published by the wife of a pastor in the capital of Alabama, she says, "Not one in a thousand of these poor creatures have any conception whatever of the sanctity of marriage."§ Even the members of Southern churches do not escape the general corruption:—"An Alabama gentleman whom I questioned with regard to the chastity of the so-called pious slaves, confessed that four negro women had borne children in his own

* Olmsted, i. 308.   † Ibid., 94.
‡ Ibid., ii. 229.   § Ibid., 225.

house, all of them at the time members in good standing of the Baptist church, and none of them calling any man husband."* "If a pastor has offspring by a woman not his wife, the church dismiss him if she is a white woman; but if she is coloured, it does not hinder his continuing to be their shepherd."†

The habitual caution imposed on clergymen and public teachers, and the necessity of apologising for the low morality of the nominally religious slaves, together with the familiarity with this immorality which all classes acquire, render the existence of a very elevated standard of morals among the whites almost an impossibility.‡

The judgment of God upon all who practise this profligacy has been thus pronounced:—"*Be not deceived: neither fornicators, nor adulterers, shall inherit the kingdom of God.*"§ "*The works of the flesh are manifest, which are these; Adultery, fornication, and such like: of the which I tell you before, that they which do such things shall not inherit the kingdom of God.*"‖ "*Murderers and whoremongers shall have their part in the lake which burneth with fire and brimstone.*"¶

But in the Slave States the law of God seems to be generally trampled on. Planters and their children, managers and overseers, rich whites and poor whites, church-members, and even some pastors, all appear by the foregoing extracts to be rotting together in licensed profligacy.

* Olmsted, ii. 226. † Linda Brent, 115. ‡ Olmsted, ii. 229.
§ 1 Cor. vi. 9, 10. ‖ Gal. v. 19-21. ¶ Rev. xxi. 8.

Nothing can prevent this while slavery lasts; because slave-holders, having the power to inflict any outrage upon women of the working-classes with impunity, they will and must be vicious. Public teachers must smile on a vice which is so general in the ruling classes. The oligarchs would never suffer their conduct to be stigmatised before their own slaves, without expelling the rash preacher who should do it. And so all that violation of the law of God which now disgraces society in the Slave States must still continue to exist, because it will not cease to be sanctioned by the silence of the ministers of religion.

It follows that those who uphold the slave system are more or less guilty of this wretchedness. The legislatures and their constituents, masters and overseers, with all who aid them to maintain their tyranny, are implicated in the guilt of corrupting the women of the working-classes. These are labouring to give them wealth, and in return they degrade them into a universal profligacy.

SECTION V.—ON CRUELTY IN THE SLAVE STATES.

The whole system of American slavery is cruel. It is cruel in law and in practice; in its principles and in its details. Slave-holders are cruel when they rob men of their liberty, forbid them to marry, and pronounce their children illegitimate,—when they separate husbands from wives, and parents from children, —when they work men and women without wages, under the whip, eleven hours a-day, from the beginning of the year to the end. But the cruelty of the system necessarily leads to many cases of special cruelty. The object of each slave-holder being to obtain from his estate as large an income as he can, he naturally seeks to secure the greatest amount of work from his labourers at the least cost. In this matter, his interest is exactly opposed to theirs. He wishes to make as much money as possible by exacting from them the greatest amount of work; and they wish to save some strength for themselves by working for him as little as possible. He looks upon them as his property; they consider that they are their own. He, as their owner, becomes self-willed, imperious, irritable; they, as under no moral obligation to work for him, and as deriving no advantage from his work, become idle and listless. They steal from him a little, because he has stolen from them much; they lie to conceal their theft, or to escape from toils which they detest; they are sullen, because he is unjust. Sometimes, when they are much tormented, they become mischievous from malice; and sometimes they attempt to run away. These tempers, acting upon his imperious nature, make him suspicious and angry. He is as ready to take offence as they are to give it; and the relation between them is one in which he seeks to conquer them by punishment, and they to wear him out by obstinacy. "The whole commerce between master and slave is a perpetual exercise of the most boisterous passions—the most unremitting despotism on the one part, and degrading submissions on the other." *

* Jefferson, in Helper, 153.

Illustrations of the violence of temper engendered by slavery meet the traveller in the Slave States very frequently. Mr Olmsted has mentioned many. To it Mr Stuart ascribes the frequent use of profane language with which he met: "The habit of lording it over the black population, and swearing at them, seems to have induced a general habit of swearing among the whites as well as the blacks, which is the more remarkable, because an oath is scarcely ever heard in the Northern States."*

At the principal hotels which Mr Stuart visited, he found the proprietors took little pains to conceal their violence. At Charleston, he stayed at the Planters' Hotel, of which he has left the following record:—
"When I returned to the hotel in the evening, I found the streets deserted. On opening the door, the male servants were, I found, laid down for the night in the passages with their clothes on. They have neither beds nor bedding; and you may kick them or tread upon them as you come in with impunity. Next morning, looking from my window, I saw Mrs Street, the landlady, give a young man such a blow behind the ear as made him reel; and I afterwards found that it was her daily and hourly practice to beat her servants, male and female, either with her fist, or with a thong made of cow-hide. Mrs Street treated all the servants in the house in the most barbarous manner; and this although she knew that Stewart, a hotel-keeper here, had lately nearly lost his life by maltreating a slave. Stewart beat his cook, who was a stout fellow, till he

* Stuart, ii. 88.

could no longer support it; he ran upon his master, and gave him such a beating that it had nearly cost him his life. The cook immediately left the house, ran off, and was never afterwards heard of; it was supposed that he had drowned himself. Not a day, however, passed without my hearing of Mrs Street whipping and ill-using her slaves. On one occasion, when one of her female slaves had disobliged her, she beat her until her own strength was exhausted, and then insisted on her bar-keeper, Mr Ferguson, proceeding to inflict the remainder of the punishment.

"I had put up my clothes in my portmanteau when I was about to set out, but finding it was rather too full, I had difficulty in getting it closed; I therefore told one of the boys to send me one of the stoutest of the men to assist me. A great robust fellow soon afterwards appeared, with tears in his eyes; he told me that just at the time when the boy called for him, he had got so sharp a blow from this devil in petticoats as had unmanned him for the moment. Upon my expressing commiseration for him, he said that about two years had elapsed since he and his wife, with his two children, had been exposed in the public market at Charleston for sale,—that he had been purchased by Mrs Street,—that his wife and children had been purchased by a different person,—and that though he was living in the same town, he was never allowed to see them; he would be beaten within an ace of his life if he ventured to go to the corner of the street. Whenever the least symptom of insubordination appears at Charleston on the part of a slave, the master sends him to the jail, where he is whipped as the master desires."*

Charleston has long been celebrated for the severity of its laws against the blacks. A dreadful case of murder occurred in Charleston in 1806. A planter called John Slater made an unoffending, unresisting slave be bound hand and foot, and compelled his companion to chop off his head and to cast his body into the waters.† For this the planter was tried, convicted, and imprisoned.

"In the month of July 1822, thirty-five slaves were executed near Charleston for an alleged conspiracy against their masters. Sixty-seven persons were convicted before a court consisting of a justice of the peace, and freeholders, without a jury. The evidence of slaves not upon oath was admitted against them, and the proof was extremely scanty."‡

"At New Orleans I got a room in the Planters' Hotel, kept by Mr Lavand; the waiters all slaves. They had no beds to sleep upon, all lying like dogs in the passages of the house. Mr Smith, the clerk of the house, told me that no evening passed on which he had not to give some of them stripes. Although I did not myself witness the master or mistress beating the slaves with barbarity, yet I heard enough to convince me that at New Orleans there are many Mrs Streets."§

* Stuart, ii. 97-109. † Ibid., 111.
‡ Ibid., 112. § Ibid., 194, 206.

We must add to this, the constant fear felt by the planters.

"Another circumstance," says Mr Godley, "which surprised me was the chronic apprehension which appears to prevail of a negro insurrection. Even here, where the whites are superior in numbers, there seems a constant feeling *incedendi per ignes*. How much stronger must such a feeling be in Carolina and Mississippi!"*

Under these circumstances slaveholders of all classes become cruel.

Foremost among the cruel is the slave-trader whose whole life is spent among the miserable creatures from whose wrongs and sufferings he gets his wealth. It is his business to tear men and women from their homes, friends, and hopes, to gratify the cupidity of slave-breeders who sell for money, and the spite of those who sell from malice. He fills his cart with children made orphans while their parents still live,—surrounds it with women who are widowed, not by nature, but by injustice,—gathers behind it men fastened by handcuffs; and then follows his gang well armed, to flog the sullen or to shoot the violent. So he travels from Virginia, the slave-breeding state, to Louisiana and Texas, the slave-consuming States.†

These men, who only sleep in safety by means of manacles and revolvers, and whose method of drying up the tears of their captives is to give them the lash, or to strike them on the mouth with the fist, are not

* Godley, ii. 208. † Shaffner, 292, 294.

likely to be men of the melting mood. It is not surprising that a woman of sense and spirit, whose brother, children, friends had all been sold to these customers of the "first families" in Virginia, should say, "I despise and detest the class of slave-traders, whom I regard as the vilest wretches on the earth."*

On the steamer between Savannah and Charleston, Mr Craft heard, through his wife, who was disguised as his sick young master, the following conversation. When the captain said, "You have a very attentive boy, sir; but you had better watch him like a hawk when you get into the North. I know several gentlemen who have lost valuable niggers among them cut-throat Abolitionists." "Sound doctrine, captain, very sound," said a rough slave-dealer, who was sitting opposite; "I would not take a nigger to the North under any consideration. I have had a deal to do with niggers in my time; but I never saw one who ever had his heel upon free soil that was worth a damn. Now, stranger, if you have made up your mind to sell that ere nigger, I am your man, mention your price." "I don't wish to sell, sir; I cannot get on well without him." "You will have to get on without him if you take him to the north. So I tell ye, stranger, you had better sell, and let me take him down to Orleans. He is a keen nigger, and I can see from the cut of his eye that he is certain to run away." "I think not, sir; I have great confidence in his fidelity." "Fie, devil! It always makes me mad to hear a man talking

* Linda Brent, 163.

of fidelity in niggers. There is not a damned one of them who would not cut sticks if he had half a chance. Cap'en, if I was the President, I would never let no man take a nigger into the North and bring him back here filled to the brim with damned abolition vices, to taint all quiet niggers with the hellish spirit of running away." *

2. *Overseers.*—A large number of plantations are under the care of overseers, while the owners live at a distance. Those overseers are the best paid who raise the largest crops; and as those raise the largest crops who flog the most, the greatest floggers are the best paid. Slave-holders must get their money; and though the cruelty of an overseer may really impoverish the owner, wearing down the labourers, causing miscarriages, and killing the weak, yet he may have so many ways of accounting for any mortality on the plantation, and so few stay long enough in one place to let the employer see the effects of their cruelty, that no considerations of that kind interfere with the administration which secures for the time the largest crops.

"Is the general character of the overseers bad?" asked Mr Olmsted of a planter. "They are the curse of this country, sir; the worst men in the community." †

Another proprietor said to Mr Olmsted of these overseers, "They are sometimes men of intelligence and piety; they are more often coarse, brutal, and licentious." ‡ "As a general rule, the larger the body

* Craft, 49.   † Olmsted, i. 53.   ‡ Ibid., 94.

of negroes, the more completely are they treated as mere property, and in accordance with a policy calculated to ensure the largest pecuniary returns."* "The chief difficulty is to overcome their great aversion to labour. If a man own many slaves therefore, the faculty which he values highest is that of making them work. Any fool could see that they were supplied with food, clothing, rest, and religious instruction." †

"Some people," said an Alabama tradesman to Mr Olmsted, "work their niggers too hard. I know a man at ———. I have had dealings with him. He has got three plantations, and he puts the hardest overseers he can get on them. He is all the time buying niggers, and they say around there that he works them to death. On these big plantations they have to use them hard to keep any sort of control over them. The overseers have always to go about armed. Their life would not be safe if they did not. As it is, they often get cut pretty bad."

"These rich men are always bidding for the overseer that will make the most cotton. If they make plenty of cotton, the owners never ask how many niggers they kill." "The fellow who can make the most cotton always gets paid the best. Overseers' wages were from two hundred dollars to three hundred dollars, but a real driving overseer would often get a thousand dollars; a real devil of an overseer would get almost any wages he would ask." ‡ "Brethren," said Mr Phillips of Jackson, Mississippi, "we must change

* Ibid., ii. 192. † Ibid. ‡ Ibid., 184, 185.

our policy. Overseers are not interested in raising children, &c. Many of them do not care whether property has deteriorated, so they have made a crop to boast of." *

"When they seek a place, they rest their claims entirely on the number of bags they have made, and generally the employer recognises the justice of the claim. No wonder he presses everything at the end of the lash; pays no attention to the sick except to keep them in the field as long as possible; and forces sucklers and breeders to the utmost. He has no other interest than to make a big crop; and if this does not please you, he knows men whom it will please." †

As those overseers are best paid who raise the largest crops, so those raise the largest crops who flog the most. The general testimony to Mr Olmsted was, "Niggers won't work unless there is somebody to drive them." ‡ "I passed," says Mr Olmsted, "the hoe-gang at work, the overseer carrying a whip,—not one looked at me; within ten minutes, I passed five who were ploughing, with no overseer in sight,—each stopped to gaze." §

"Overseers are changed every year; a few remain four or five years, but the average time that they remain on the same plantation does not exceed two years." ‖ "I should judge that a large majority of

---

* Olmsted, ii. 187.
† Southern Agriculturist, in Olmsted, ii., 188.
‡ See ii. 121, &c. &c. § Ibid., 95; see 178.
‖ Southern Agriculturist, Olmsted, ii. 182.

all the slaves in the district (Mississippi) were left by their owners to the nearly unlimited government of hireling overseers the greater part of the time."*
"About one-half the slaves of Louisiana, and one-third that of Mississippi, belong to estates of not less than fifty slaves each; and of these I believe nine-tenths live in plantations which their owners reside upon, if at all, transiently." † Of all these estates overseers alone have charge; and "it is apparent that as the testimony of negroes against them would not be received as evidence in court, there is very little probability that any excessive severity would be restrained by fear of the law." ‡

I will only cite one instance of the discipline by which overseers get good crops for their employers. On one of the tributaries of the Mississippi, Mr Olmsted visited an estate while the owner, who generally lived on another property, happened to be there. The estate, comprehending four plantations, with more than a hundred persons on each, was under a manager and four overseers. With the manager Mr Olmsted rode over a part of the estate. In a cabin which they entered lay a woman groaning. The manager having felt her pulse, and looked at her tongue, said, "Just get up and go to the field; and if you don't work smart, you'll get a dressing. Do you hear?" Afterwards meeting with the overseer, he said, "There's that girl Caroline, there is nothing the matter with her, except she is sore with the whipping she got. You

---

* Olmsted, ii., 232.   † Ibid., 233.   ‡ Ibid., 195.

must go and get her out. We have to be sharp with them," he added to Mr Olmsted; "if we were not, every negro on the estate would be a-bed." She had been delivered of a dead child about six weeks before. Since that had been flogged, and now was likely to be flogged again.* The hoe-gangs were driven to their work by a powerful negro, who walked in the rear cracking his whip. "The whip was evidently in constant use. 'It must be disagreeable,' I said to one of the overseers, 'to have to punish them so much as you do.' 'It's my business, and I think nothing of it. Why, sir, I would not mind killing a nigger more than I would a dog. Some negroes are determined never to let a white man whip them, and will resist you when you attempt it. Of course, you must kill them in that case.' Once a negro, whom he was about to whip, struck at his head with a hoe. He tried to shoot him, but the pistol missing fire, he rushed in and knocked him down with the butt end of it. At another time, a negro whom he was punishing threatened him; he went to the house for his gun; as he was returning the negro ran; he fired at once, and put six buckshot into his hips. He always carried a bowie-knife, and he kept a pair of pistols ready loaded over the mantel-piece." †

While one of the overseers on this estate was shewing Mr Olmsted over his plantation the following incident occurred:—"In going from one side of it to the other we had thrice crossed a deep gully, at the bottom

* Olmsted, ii. 193, 200. † Ibid., 202, 203.

of which was a thick covert of brushwood. We were crossing it a third time when the overseer suddenly stopped his horse, exclaiming, 'What's that! Hallo, who are you there?' 'Sam's Sall, sir.' 'What are you skulking there for?' The girl half rose, but gave no answer. 'Have you been here all day?' 'No, sir.' 'How did you get here?' No reply. After some further questioning, she said her father accidentally locked her in when he went out in the morning. 'How did you manage to get out?' 'Pushed a plank off, and crawled out.' 'That won't do; come out here.' The girl arose at once and walked to him. She was about eighteen years of age. A bunch of keys hung at her waist. 'Your father locked you in, but you have got the keys, that won't do; get down.' The girl knelt on the ground. He got off his horse, and holding him with his left hand, struck her thirty or forty blows across the shoulders with his raw-hide whip—a terrible instrument. They were well laid on, at arm's length. At every stroke the girl winced, and exclaimed, 'Oh, sir,' or 'Please, sir;' not groaning nor screaming. At length he stopped and said, 'Now tell me the truth.' The girl repeated the same story. 'You have not got enough yet,' said he; 'pull up your clothes—lie down.' The girl drew closely all her garments under her shoulders, and lay down upon the ground with her face toward the overseer, who continued to flog her with the raw hide across her naked loins and thighs with as much strength as before. She now shrunk away from him, not rising, but writhing and screaming, 'Oh, don't, sir! oh, please stop, master! please, sir! please, sir! oh, that's enough, master! O Lord! O master, master! O God, master. Do stop! O God, master! O God!' A young gentleman of fifteen was with us; he had ridden in front, and now, turning on his horse, looked back with an expression of impatience at the delay. It was the first time I had ever seen a woman flogged. I glanced again at the grim business-like face of the overseer, and again at the young gentleman, who had evidently not the faintest sympathy with my emotion. The screaming yells and the whip-strokes had ceased when I reached the top of the bank; choking, sobbing, spasmodic groans only were heard. My young companion met me there, and immediately after the overseer. He laughed as he joined us, and said, 'She meant to cheat me out of a day's work.' 'Was it necessary to punish her so severely?' 'Oh yes, (laughing again;) if I hadn't, she would have done the same thing again to-morrow; and half the people on the plantation would have followed her example. They would never do any work if they were not afraid of being whipped.' We soon afterward met an old man who, on being closely questioned, said that he had seen the girl leave the gang as they went to work after dinner. It appeared that she had been at work during the forenoon; but at dinner-time the gang was moved; and as it passed through the gully, she slipped out. The driver had not missed her. It was a red-hot experience to me."*

* Olmsted, ii. 204.

A young girl whom God made to be free, loved, and happy, but who, robbed of happiness and liberty, was worked daily eleven hours under a driver, longed with an irresistible desire for half a day's rest from the hoe and the whip. After working half a day for a tyrant without remuneration, she took for herself a few hours which were her own. For this short rest from a toil unfitted to her sex, and for which she was paid nothing, she received thirty blows upon her shoulders without a murmur; and then being forced to lie down naked in the presence of a youth and two men, was flogged upon her stomach and her thighs by the torturing ox-hide till she screamed out in agony. Blow after blow fell on the meek victim, who groaned, writhed, screamed, sobbed, and cried for mercy. Blow after blow tortured, wealed, and scarred her body for snatching half a day's rest from a life of compulsory toil. "The manner of the overseer and his subsequent conversation about it, indicated that it was by no means unusual in severity."* All those screams and groans were nothing to him, because he was familiar with them. That brutality was not the effect of passion, but was part of his system of government. Had he thought it cruel, he would not have inflicted it before a stranger. Nothing but complete familiarity with such sights could make him forget that Mr Olmsted must writhe under his lashes almost as much as the girl whom he was torturing. The apathy of the planter's son can only be explained in the same manner. He

* Ibid., ii. 204.

had so often seen girls flogged that he could not be moved by it. Besides, the manager and the master were both then on the estate. Could the overseer have inflicted that torture on the poor girl in the presence of Mr Olmsted, and then have laughed at it, unless he had known that both of them would approve of it as a salutary discipline? Mr Olmsted might speak of it to both, but both the "poetic" manager and the princely planter would pronounce it to be necessary. The planter must have his cotton; the manager must get it for him; and every girl on the estate must be flogged with equal severity rather than that the crop should be diminished. There was nothing to prevent that cruelty being inflicted any day by that overseer upon any one of the hundred labourers under his lash. There is nothing to hinder the thousands of overseers, whom slaveholders themselves have represented as worthless and cruel, from even surpassing it in cruelty. The planters pay them in proportion to the work which they can extort from their trembling gangs; and whatever may be the amount of flogging by which they extort it, the law affords them perfect impunity.

Besides wishing to lighten their compulsory toils, negroes are tempted to take from their master some part of that which they think he has stolen from them. Thefts of this sort are of constant occurrence. "Everywhere on the plantations the notion has become a fixed point of the negro system of ethics, that the result of labour belongs of right to the labourer; and on this ground even the religious feel justified in using massa's property for their own benefit. They almost universally pilfer from the household stores when they have a safe opportunity."* But this practice must tempt masters to defend themselves with a fierceness proportioned to their danger. What part of their property will be safe if their servants may take it without the sense of guilt and without the fear of punishment? Thefts are, therefore, likely to be punished as they were in the two following instances:—"Two (slaves) were detected; a ham and some liquor being found in their huts. They were summoned by their master. No words were used, but a club felled them to the ground. A rough box was their coffin. Nothing was said."† "Another slave who stole a pig to appease his hunger was flogged. In desperation he tried to run away. At the end of two miles he was so faint with loss of blood, he thought he was dying. Too sick to walk, he crept back on his hands and knees. When he reached his master's, it was night. He had not strength to rise and open the gate. He moaned and tried to call for help. I had a friend living in the same family. She went out and found the prostrate man at the gate. She and two men carried him in, and laid him on the floor. The back of his shirt was one clot of blood. The master said he deserved a hundred more lashes."‡ How many of these floggings and murders are going on in the Slave States every day?

In some cases, similar cruelties take place upon slight provocation. Mr Conant's servant gave him

* Olmsted, I. 106.   † Linda Brent, 72.   ‡ Ibid., 73.

some offence. "He was whipped, and tied to a tree in front of the house. It was a stormy night in winter; a member of the family fearing that he might freeze to death, begged that he might be taken down, but the master would not relent. He remained there three hours, and when he was cut down, he was more dead than alive." *

Jealousy often adds to the rage of the slaveholder. The master of Linda Brent was furious at learning that another presumed to love her. "The next morning," she relates, "a message was brought to me, 'Master wants you in his study.' 'So you want to be married, do you?' said he. 'Yes, sir.' 'Well, I'll soon convince you whether I am your master. Do you love this nigger?' 'Yes, sir.' 'How dare you tell me so?' He sprung on me like a tiger, and gave me a stunning blow. There was a silence some minutes. Finally he asked, 'Do you know that I have a right to do as I like with you—that I can kill you if I please? Many masters would have killed you on the spot. Never let me hear that fellow's name mentioned again. If I ever know of your speaking to him, I will cowhide you both; and if I catch him lurking about my premises, I will shoot him." †

"A planter had a favourite among his girls, and suspecting that she was unduly kind to one of his men, he mutilated him. There was not sufficient testimony to convict him, but everybody believes he was guilty." ‡

* Linda Brent, 73. † Ibid., 60. ‡ Olmsted, i. 356.

Women, too, are sometimes furious through jealousy, when the rage which should attack the adulterous husband falls on his helpless victim.

"I once saw a young slave-girl dying soon after the birth of a child nearly white. In her agony she cried out, 'O Lord, take me!' Her mistress stood by and mocked at her like an incarnate fiend: "You suffer, do you? I am glad of it.' The poor mother turned away sobbing. Her dying daughter called her feebly; and as she bent over her, I heard her say, 'Don't grieve so: mother, God knows all about it, and He will have mercy on me.'"*

"A negress was hung this year, in Alabama, for the murder of her child. At her trial, she said her owner was the father of her child; and that her mistress treated it so cruelly in consequence, that she had killed it to save it from further suffering."† Poor girl, she was seduced by a ruffian whose power she could not resist, ill-treated herself, driven to desperation by the cruelty practised on her child, and then hung without pity; while the real murderer, the sneaking seducer, who would not defend the girl whom he had ruined, triumphed in his impunity. God's word is, that murderers and adulterers shall have their part in the lake of fire, (Rev. xxi. 8;) and he was both. But how many slave-girls at this moment are suffering in a similar manner from profligate slaveholders, and from their furious wives?

I must pass over, for the sake of brevity, many re-

* Linda Brent, 24. † Olmsted, i. 308.

volting instances of cruelty to fugitives. When a man runs away, he becomes so troublesome, so bad an example to his fellow-labourers, and so worthless for sale, that no motives of self-interest interfere with the exercise of his master's fury towards him. Runaways are hunted, their flesh is torn by blood-hounds, they are imprisoned, ironed, starved, flogged; and when they resist, are shot.

But the heaviest punishments are reserved for those who, under any circumstances, take the life of a white man. At a house where Mr Olmsted lodged, the mistress thus expounded her views of justice to negroes:—"Why, over to Fanin, there was a negro woman that killed her mistress with an axe, and her two little ones. The people just flocked together, and hung her right upon the spot. They ought to have piled some wood round her, and burned her to death." *

In this opinion, she was by no means singular. Not long since, a man having murdered his master, was roasted at a slow fire in the presence of many thousand slaves, driven to the ground from all the adjoining counties. There magistrates and clergymen addressed appropriate warnings to the assembled subjects. †

"After the burning of a negro near Knoxville, a few years ago, the deed was justified as necessary for the maintenance of order." The local paper (the *Whig*) used the following language:—"We have to say

* Olmsted, ii. 13. † Ibid., 348.

in defence of the act, that it was not perpetrated by an excited multitude, but by one thousand citizens, who were cool, calm, and deliberate." The editor, who is a Methodist preacher, adds, "The punishment was unequal to the crime. Had we been there, we should have taken a part, and even suggested the pinching of pieces out of him with red-hot pincers, the cutting off of a limb at a time, and then burning them all in a heap." How much more horrible than the deed are these apologies for it! Doubtless, this reverend gentleman expresses the feeling of the ruling mind of his community. Would a similar provocation have developed a similar spirit in any other nominally Christian people?

"Constantly, and everywhere through all the South are there occurrences of this significance: I do not say as horrible, though I can answer for it, that no year in the last ten has passed without something as bad." "The late Judge Jay told me that he had evidence in his possession of negro-burnings every year in the last twenty." *

"There are, Heaven knows, vicious and tyrannical institutions in ample abundance on the earth. But this institution is the only one of them all which requires to keep it going that human beings should be burned alive. What must American slavery be if deeds like these are necessary under it? If they are not necessary, and are yet done, is not the evidence against slavery still more damning? The South are in rebel-

* Ibid., ii. 351-354.

lion, not for simple slavery; they are in rebellion for the right of burning human creatures alive." *

SECTION VI.—CONCEALMENT OF CRIMES.

We have seen that the slave-holder may legally commit many crimes; but beside all these, he may perpetrate with impunity cruelties beyond all that can be known or imagined to gratify his passion or his pride, his jealousy, his hatred, his revenge, or his fear. The law forbids him to overwork his slaves; but he can work them till they drop down dead, and he may go unquestioned. An overseer made to Mr Olmsted the following statement respecting himself:—"There was a nigger one day at Mr ———'s who said he could not work. I thought it was nothing but damned sulkiness; so I paddled him and made him go to work; but in two days he was under ground." Who asks an owner about such murders? † The law forbids him *maliciously* to deprive his servants of life; but he may work, or flog, or starve them to death, and no one ask anything about it.‡

The law forbids him to mutilate them; but he can do it without fear of punishment.§ He can with perfect impunity dash out their brains for a petty theft, or he may shoot them for running away, without exposing himself to any inconvenience.‖

---

* *Fraser's Magazine*, Feb. 1862, 264.
† Olmsted, i. 120. ‡ Linda Brent, 75.
§ Olmsted, i. 356. ‖ Linda Brent, 78, 76.

If he can do all this safely, why may he not with equal impunity do anything else which a fiendish ingenuity may suggest? What avails it that the law forbids? Should he select a barn or a cellar, or any place where his slaves may guard the approach, and gag his victim, so that no sound may reach a distant ear, fifty slaves might witness a murder, and not dare to whisper a word about it. "The secrets of slavery," says Linda Brent, "are concealed like those of the Inquisition."* Whatever may be the injustice which any slaveholder may commit against his servants, no one can know it.

"A slave cannot be a witness in the case of a white man." If a wife see her husband murdered by his master, or if she be forcibly taken from her husband, she cannot complain to any magistrate. If a man lose his wife, his children, his bed, his clothes, if he be starved till he is a walking skeleton, or beaten till he is covered from head to foot with bleeding wounds, he can appeal to no court of justice. Should a black witness fifty murders in a plantation, he cannot be called as a witness to one of them.†

"I was told here," (Cooper's River, South Carolina,) "on authority which seemed to be quite unquestionable—that of a wealthy planter who lived in this neighbourhood—that a planter whose estate is at no great distance from the high road which I was travelling, was in the habit of punishing his slaves by putting them in coffins which were partly nailed down;

* Linda Brent, 55. † Shaffner, 299.

H

and that this punishment had again and again resulted in the death of the slaves. The punishment was inflicted only in the presence of slaves, whose evidence was inadmissible. He added that the coffins had been seen, that the slaves who it was said had lost their lives had disappeared, and that no doubt was entertained that their deaths had been occasioned by their being shut up in coffins. The same person works his slaves on Sundays, though contrary to law, taking care that no white man sees them."*

What slave will speak of any cruelty which he has seen, when his evidence would be in the sight of the law nothing, and in the judgment of his master a capital offence! A slave-holder may therefore commit any crime against a slave, with the certainty that it will be unpunishable, because his slaves may not testify against him, and in most cases white men cannot. Even if white men could, they would not, the *ésprit de corps* and self-love forbidding. This was thus explained to Mr Olmsted:—"Suppose you are my neighbour: if you maltreat your negroes, and I see it, am I going to prefer charges against you to the magistrates? I might possibly get you punished according to law; but if I did or did not, I should have you and your family, and friends far and near, for my mortal enemies."†

Besides, whatever evidence might be produced against a white man on behalf of a black man would be useless; because a white judge and a white jury, backed

* Stuart, ii. 85.   † Olmsted, ii. 47.

by a white mob, would refuse to condemn him, however clear the law, and however certain the facts; while officials would not punish one of their own fraternity. Yet, in the face of all these facts, Colonel Shaffner says, "The laws of all the Southern States are very complete in the protection of the slave."* How can an author of character advance such an assertion! The laws themselves are outrageously cruel, and those which seem protections are a solemn mockery —a mere veil thrown over gross oppression. If a white man commit any felony against his slave, no advocate will plead against him, no witness will give testimony, no jury will convict, no judge will condemn. Black men may not condemn him, white men will not, and the felon will triumph whatever the enormity of his crime. If romances are written about the patriarchal simplicity of the slave-holder, and the childlike gaiety of his slaves, who can believe them?

A Major-General, who visited a lady in the South, wrote home thus:—"We hunt, ride, fish, pay morning visits, play chess, read, or lounge till dinner, which is delicately cooked. Then till bed-time, we sing, play whist, or coquet. It is a charming life. The slaves appear to be in a manner free, yet are obedient and polite. They are a happy, careless, unreflecting, good-natured race, who, left to themselves, would degenerate into drones or brutes, but subjected to wholesome restraint become the best and most contented of labourers." †

* Shaffner, 291. † Ibid., 302.

"Such a traveller," says Linda Brent, "assures people that he has seen slavery for himself, that the slaves don't want their freedom. What does *he* know of the half-starved wretches toiling from dawn to dark on the plantations,—of mothers shrieking for their children, torn from their arms by slave-traders,—of young girls dragged down into moral filth;—of pools of blood round the whipping-post,—of hounds trained to tear human flesh,—of men screwed into cotton-presses to die! The slave-holder shewed him none of these things, and the slaves dared not tell of them if he had asked them."*

Let the apologists of slavery say what they will, irresponsible power placed in the hands of wicked men, with the power of absolute concealment, must occasion innumerable villanies. Planters interested to hide each enormity in a system which fills their purses, multiplies their pleasures, and exalts their dignity, are witnesses too partial to be credited. Travellers flattered and fêted by them, who are welcomed to baronial mansions, witness agreeable manners, drink excellent wines, and taste nothing but the sweets of slavery, can know nothing of its crimes. Planters will not parade before them the excesses of their lusts, or their acts of rage. But against all this unreliable testimony there are probabilities so strong, and facts so damning, that we are obliged to disbelieve it. Why, if the masters are so good and the slaves so happy, is the power of the owner made so absolute, and the concealment of

* Linda Brent, 114.

his crimes so complete? Why may the injured never sigh out even a meek complaint against the oppressor? Why is the whole South in conspiracy to gag the poor bondsman, that he might not utter to those in authority a single prayer for mercy, though his body may be torn by the lash, and his heart breaking with his sorrow? Why is there so impenetrable a veil thrown over this paradise? Why are Abolitionists likely to be shot if they ever cross a plantation without a permit? There is a feverishness about Southern society which does not look as if all parties were contented. Besides, such horrors now and then come out of the obscurity. Men are burned by slow fires, before exulting crowds, while magistrates and clergymen attend to give them solemn sanction. Even since the rebellion five men have been burned in Alabama, and two at Savannah; religious men have come to General Phelps, loaded with chains, or sore with stripes; freemen trying to escape from the slave region, have been seized, fastened in upright coffins, and shot as felons; and eighteen freemen have been hung for having in their possession a copy of Mr Lincoln's Proclamation of Emancipation. If these things come out, what must there be within that region which is as dark and as silent as hell? Who can tell what cursing and raging, what flogging and starving, what ironing, maiming, shooting, and burning may be going on all through the slave territory, especially now, when slave-holders are dreading an insurrection which they know that they have provoked, and when they see, as they think, in their slaves, enemies who can only be restrained by a strong, unremitting, remorseless, and crushing exercise of power?

SECTION VII.—OPPOSITION TO RELIGIOUS INSTRUCTION.

The slave-holders have made their system as strong as law can make it. We have seen that the master's power over his labourers is absolute. He can flog them till his ox-hide is soaked in their blood for anything or nothing,—he may torture them in any other way which malice may suggest, short of mutilation,—he may sell them away from his plantation,—if they resist his violence, he may kill them,—and should his brutality lead him to indulge in any excess of cruelty which the law would notice, he is safe, for not one of them may bear witness against any crime which he may commit.

Yet all these safeguards would be incomplete, if they, the slave-holders, allowed their labourers to get knowledge. Tyrants usually hate knowledge and virtue in those whom they oppress. As able men detect their crimes, and virtuous men condemn them, they usually oppose the acquirement of knowledge and the exercise of conscience. The slave-holders, aware of their danger from this cause, have taken measures to avert it.

To rivet their chains more completely upon their labourers, they have kept them in brutish ignorance. Those who are to be worked as brutes must be hindered from thinking as men. Of course, negroes, sprung from the same parents with ourselves, are as capable of improvement as any other part of the race, and will doubtless in the course of time, when free, educated, and religious, manifest all the capacities of free Englishmen or free Anglo-Saxon Americans. Already, in the Slave States and elsewhere, many have shewn intelligence and aptitude of improvement. But these very indications have forced upon their masters the necessity of keeping them in ignorance.

I. Slave-holders have set themselves against the oral instruction of their labourers. The gospel is necessary for their salvation.* Like ourselves, they must be saved by grace through faith;† and faith comes by hearing.‡ It is the will of our Saviour that all men should hear; for His disciples have received from Him this order, "*Go ye into all the world, and preach the gospel to every creature.*"§ What Christians are to make known to all men, all men have a right to hear; and the slave has, therefore, an absolute, inalienable right to hear how he may be saved. But slave-holders have withheld from him that right.

In 1800, an Act was passed in South Carolina, "That assemblies of slaves, free negroes, mulattoes, and a portion of white persons, met together for the purpose of mental instruction in a confined and secret place, are declared to be an unlawful meeting; and the magistrates are required to enter, to break open the doors, if their entrance is resisted, and to disperse the said

---

* John xvii. 1, 2.
† John iii. 16, vi. 47; Luke vii. 50; Acts xvi. 31; Eph. ii. 8.
‡ Rom. x. 13-17. § Mark xvi. 15.

persons; and they may inflict such corporal punishment, not exceeding twenty lashes, upon such slaves, free negroes, white persons, &c., as they may find necessary for deterring them from such unlawful assemblage in future."* According to this law, any minister or other Christian who, being hindered by mob violence from preaching the gospel to working-men in public, gathers a few of them into his house to preach it to them, may be flogged for it.

In 1821, the City Council of Charleston, South Carolina, passed the following:—

"That the marshal be instructed to inform the ministers of the gospel, and others who keep night and Sunday schools for slaves, that the education of such persons is prohibited by law, and that the City Council feel bound to enforce the penalty against those who may hereafter forfeit the same." †

In Virginia, the revised code of 1819 declares, "That all meetings of slaves, or free negroes, or mulattoes, mixing with the slaves at any meeting-house in the night, shall be deemed an unlawful assembly; and any justice of the peace may issue his warrant to any sworn officer, authorising him to disperse the said assembly, and to inflict corporal punishment on the offenders at the discretion of any justice of the peace, not to exceed twenty lashes." ‡ Twenty lashes may be inflicted on any Christian negroes who, being prevented by cruel masters from hearing the gospel by day, should at night obey the direction of the apostle by "not forsak-

---

* Shaffner, 231. † Ibid. ‡ Ibid., 281, 282.

ing the assembling of themselves together" for the exposition of the Word of God and prayer.*

Kentucky, Maryland, Delaware, "all have laws forbidding the unlawful assembling of slaves, free negroes, and mulattoes. The laws cited may be considered as positive prohibitions to the slaves and free negroes holding or attending religious meetings. The language is plain, and the penalties affixed are severe."†

Each wicked slave-holder may act upon these laws, and hinder his slaves from attending meetings for preaching and prayer. Other laws increase his power. Of course, he can hinder all preaching on his own estate;‡ but further, if there is any religious meeting near his estate, he can hinder his labourers from attending it: "The master can restrict their attendance at meetings."§ If a man leave his master's plantation without a pass, he is liable to be flogged. "The pass generally reads thus: 'To the Gentlemen Patrol.—My servant John has permission to visit the plantation of Mr Jones, and to return home by ten o'clock to-night.' This pass must be signed by the master, overseer, or some member of the owner's family. The patrol is composed of some two, three, or more men, who go from plantation to plantation to see if there are any unlawful assemblings of the slaves. If they find a slave from another plantation without a pass, he is whipped." ||

Mr Watson, a slave-holder, mentioned to Mr Olmsted

* Heb. x. 25.   † Shaffner, 282, 223.   ‡ Olmsted, ii., 212.
§ Shaffner, 280. || Ibid., 286.

a "very religious lady," who worked her slaves from half-past three every morning to nearly nine at night. If they were not dressed clean on Sundays, they were whipped. They were never allowed to go off the plantation; and if they were caught speaking to a negro from any other place, they were whipped.*

"In Georgia, and I believe in all the Slave States, a white has the power to question any coloured person, particularly at night and on Sundays, without a written pass. If the coloured person refuses to answer, he may be beaten; his defending himself makes him an outlaw; and if he be killed on the spot, the murderer will be exempted from all blame."†

In extenuation of this legal cruelty, Colonel Shaffner says, "Although these laws may seem to be barbarously severe, they are not practically carried out, except where there is a suspicion of danger. We know that they are not rigidly enforced." "For many years it has been the policy of the slave-holding States to encourage religious instruction among the slaves."‡ But I fear that here, as elsewhere, his affection for the slave-holders leads him to overlook the evidence which is against them. A majority of the public houses of worship at the South are small, rude structures of logs or rough boards, built by the united labour or contributions of the people of a district, and are used as places of assembly for all public purposes. "Few of them have any regular clergymen, but preachers of different de-

---

* Olmsted, ii. 100.   † Craft, 39.
‡ Shaffner, 283, 284.

nominations go from one to another in rotation. The proportion of ministers, of all sorts, to people is estimated at one to thirteen hundred."* White preachers being few, on almost every large plantation, and in every neighbourhood of small ones, there is one man who has come to be considered the head or pastor of the local church. The self-respect of the preacher is often increased by the consideration in which he is held by his master.† Most of these must be illiterate; but some, I doubt not, are like Andrew Brian, upon whose grave-stone at Savannah the following words are inscribed:—" Sacred to the memory of Andrew Brian, pastor of the First Coloured Baptist Church in Savannah. Though he laboured under many disadvantages, yet he has done more good among the poor slaves than all the learned doctors in America. He was imprisoned for the gospel, was severely whipped; but, while under the lash, told his prosecutor he rejoiced not only to be whipped, but to suffer death for the cause of Christ. He continued preaching the gospel until 6th October 1812. He was an honour to human nature, an ornament to religion, and a friend to mankind. This stone is erected by the church as a token of love for their most faithful pastor, A.D. 1821."‡

This practice of whipping men for preaching Christ is not yet obsolete:—" While in North Carolina, I heard of two recent occasions in which public religious services had been interrupted, and the preachers—very

* Olmsted, i. 261.   † Ibid., 260.
‡ Ibid., 226.

estimable coloured men—publicly whipped."* Planters sometimes assured Mr Olmsted that the negro preachers were the worst characters among them;† but this might be because they were bad men themselves. "The world hateth me," said Jesus, "because I testify of it that the works thereof are evil," (John vii. 7.)

But if the planters dislike negro preachers, they should encourage white ones; which, indeed, Colonel Shaffner asserts that they do. Some may; but certainly not all. A planter and his manager, who assured Mr Olmsted that the preachers "were the most dishonest slaves on the plantation, and oftenest required punishment," (so that the way that they encouraged preaching was to whip the preachers,) added, "They did not like to have white men preach on the estate; and in future they did not intend to permit them to do so."‡ Nor was this wealthy proprietor peculiar in his opinion:—"Among the wealthier slave-owners, and in all those parts of the country where the enslaved portion of the population outnumbers the whites, there is generally a visible and often an avowed distrust of the effect of religious exercises upon slaves; and even the preaching of white clergymen to them is permitted by many with reluctance." §

When it is reluctantly permitted, it is jealously watched. In Louisiana, "if any one use incendiary language, in the pulpit or elsewhere, with the view to

---

* Olmsted, i. 226.   † Ibid., ii. 212.   ‡ Ibid.
§ Ibid., ii. 213.

excite the slaves to discontent and insurrection, he is guilty of felony, and may be punished by imprisonment or death." * Threatenings of this kind must materially embarrass ministers in preaching. "I have not," says Mr Olmsted, "been able to resist the impression that, even when the economy, safety, and duty of some sort of religious education of the slaves is conceded, so much caution, reservation, and restriction is felt to be necessary in their instruction, that the result, in the majority of cases, has been merely to furnish a delusive clothing of Christian forms and phrases to the original vague superstition of the African savage." † Many of the Southern preachers have become advocates of the slave system, like Mr Palmer of New Orleans; Bible defences of it have been written and circulated; ‡ and ministers preach on its behalf. Such preachers the slave-holders encourage, but they can do no good among the slaves. Even faithful white ministers are not trusted by the negroes as their friends.

An excellent Presbyterian minister, employed by the slave-holders in the county of Liberty, in Georgia, to teach their slaves,—a fact which Mr Olmsted declares to be "almost unparalleled,"—after labouring thirteen years among them, thus addressed his patrons:— "The current of conversation and of business, in respect to negroes, runs in the channel of interest, and thus increases the insensibility of owners. This custom of society acts on the negroes, who, seeing,

* Shaffner, 282.   † Olmsted, ii. 214.   ‡ Ibid., i. 316.

feeling, and knowing that their owners regard them as their money only, are inclined to lose sight of their higher interests, and to estimate themselves, religion, and virtue no higher than their owners do. The consequent mingling up of husbands and wives, children and youths, banishes the privacy and modesty essential to domestic purity, and opens wide the door to profligacy. If family relations are not protected, we cannot look for any considerable degree of moral and religious improvement. One of the chief causes of the immorality of negroes arises from the indifference of themselves and of their owners to family relations." *
One remarkable case occurred in South Carolina. The Rev. T. Tupper, a Methodist minister, who had been chosen by the Conference of that State to preach to slaves, "because he was a cautious and discreet person, who would confine himself to verbal instruction," was obliged by the enmity of the planters to retire. Three hundred and fifty of the leading planters and citizens signed a remonstrance, in which they stated, " Verbal instruction will increase the desire of the black population to learn. Open the missionary sluice, and the current will swell in its onward advance. We thus expect a progressive system of improvement will be introduced, which, if not checked, will ultimately revolutionise our civil institutions." Mr Tupper retired; and *The Greenville Mountaineer*, in announcing his withdrawal, stated, "that the great body of the people were opposed to the religious instruction of their

* Olmsted, ii. 216.

slaves, even if it were given orally."* "Such a formal, distinct, and effective manifestation of sentiment, made by so important a portion of the slave-holding body, cannot be supposed to represent a merely local or occasional state of mind."†

II. Let us now see how the slave legislatures have promoted the reading of the Word of God. This is one of the most inestimable blessings which God has given us. It is the great means through which we are saved. For we are saved by grace through faith, (Eph. ii. 8.) He who believes in Jesus as his Saviour from sin and hell is saved; he who believes not in Him is condemned, (John iii. 16-18; Mark xvi. 16.) "*He who believeth on the Son hath everlasting life; he who believeth not the Son shall not see life, but the wrath of God abideth on him,*" (John iii. 36.) But faith can only be obtained through knowledge, (John xvii. 1, 2;) and the knowledge of Jesus is obtained through the Word of God, (Rom. x. 17.) By it God converts men from unbelief to faith, from sin to godliness, (James i. 18.) It is the appointed means of regeneration, (1 Pet. i. 23;) it is more likely to convert the reader to God than the sight of a person returned from the heavenly world to tell us of its joys, (Luke xvi. 31;) and through it God forms the character of His servants, (John xvii. 17.) It is the sword which God the Spirit has put into our hands to defend ourselves from all evil, (Eph. vi. 17;) the disciples of Jesus are urged by Him and by His apostles to read it con-

* Ibid., ii. 214. † Ibid.

stantly, (John v. 39, Eph. vi. 17, Col. iii. 16, 1 Pet. ii. 1, 2, &c., &c.;) and God has promised His blessing to those who do, (Ps. i., xix., cxix.; Deut. vi. 6-9; Josh. i. 8, &c., &c.) Yet the slave-holders have forbidden their labourers to read this book. To all of us who believe in Jesus it is invaluable. We read it constantly; it is our guide in duty, and our support in trial; it contains the revelation of our Saviour, and tells us the mind and will of God. Like David, we value it more than gold, and think it sweeter than honey. Adapted for every class, it is especially capable of cheering afflicted believers; teaching them to look through all the troubles of their lot upward to God who pities them, and onward to heaven where they will soon be happy. Yet this book the slaveholders have forbidden to the working-classes, by forbidding them to read at all. "In nearly all the slave-holding States there are laws forbidding the education of slaves."

In 1740, the colony of South Carolina passed a law, that "every person who shall teach a slave to write shall forfeit one hundred pounds." In 1821, the City Council of Charleston passed the following:—"That the marshal be instructed to inform the ministers of the gospel, and others who keep night and Sunday schools for slaves, that the education of such persons is prohibited by law." In Virginia, the revised code of 1819 declares, "That all meetings of slaves or free negroes at any school for teaching them to read or write shall be deemed an unlawful assembly; and any justice of the peace may issue his warrant to disperse the said assembly, and to inflict corporal punishment on the offenders, not to exceed twenty lashes."

"In North Carolina, to teach a slave to read is punished with thirty-nine lashes, if the offender be a free negro, and if a white man, then with a fine of 200 dollars."

"In Georgia, to teach a free negro or slave is punished by a fine of 500 dollars. If the teacher be a coloured man, he may be fined or whipped."

"In Louisiana it is felony to teach slaves to read, and the penalty is one year's imprisonment." *

These laws are not inoperative. Mr and Mrs Craft never had an opportunity of learning to read before they made their escape. In Sunday-schools for the slaves reading is not taught. Linda Brent has related her teaching of an old slave in the following terms:—
"I knew an old black man whose piety and childlike trust in God were beautiful to witness. He thought he should know how to serve God better if he could only read the Bible. He came to me and begged me to teach him. I asked him if he did not know that it was contrary to law, and that slaves were whipped for teaching each other to read. This brought the tears into his eyes." However, the law was braved; a time and place were chosen, so as to secure secrecy; and the old man at length began to read. After spelling a few words, he said, "'Honey, it 'pears to me when I can read dis good book, I shall be nearer to God. I

* Shaffner, 280–282.

only wants to read dis book dat I may know how to live; den I hab no fear about dying." At the end of six months he had read through the New Testament. "One day I said, 'Uncle Fred, how do you manage to get your lessons so well?' 'You nebber gibs me a lesson dat I don't pray to God to help me to understan' what I reads; and He does help me, chile.' There are thousands who, like good Uncle Fred, are thirsting for the water of life; but the law forbids it, and the churches withhold it."* Colonel Shaffner, in his youth, much to his credit, broke the law by teaching some slaves to read;† but since that the slave-holders have apparently become more vigilant. "Mrs Douglas, a Virginia woman, was tried, convicted, and punished a year or two since for teaching a number of slaves to read contrary to law."‡ Her sentence was, to be imprisoned in the county jail (Norfolk, Virginia) for a month, and to pay the costs of the prosecution.§

It is no answer to this to allege that there are a number of Sunday-schools in the South, because in those schools reading is not taught; and they may be encouraged, because it gives the teachers the opportunity of repeating to the scholars, from January to December, from the New Testament, these sentences: —"*Slaves, obey in all things your masters according to the flesh,*" (Col. iii. 22.) "*Slaves, be subject to your masters with all fear,*" (1 Pet. ii. 18.)

* Linda Brent, 111–113. † Shaffner, 287.
‡ Olmsted, i. 307. § Craft, 35–37.

The "eminent divine," indeed, who has written on the "Law of Servitude," asserts that "in family after family the daughters of slave-owners are employed, especially on Sunday, in teaching servants to read. In no land but England can so large a class read for themselves the Word of God."

He is speaking chiefly of Louisiana; but "in Louisiana it is felony to teach slaves to read, and the penalty is one year's imprisonment."[*] If there are some young ladies in the South brave enough to do an act of charity at the cost of being branded as felons, it is to be feared that these gentle felons are few. If there are, as the "eminent divine" asserts, many slaves who can read, they have doubtless, like old Frederick, braved flogging, and learned from their fellow-slaves.

Slave-holders have many motives to keep a knowledge of the Bible from their servants, because in it God so plainly condemns them. What must slaves think when they read the following passages?—

"*He that stealeth a man, and selleth him, or if he be found in his hand, he shall surely be put to death,*" (Exod. xxi. 16.) That is what each Virginian gentleman does who breeds and sells slaves.

"*Woe unto him that useth his neighbour's service without wages, and giveth him not for his work,*" (Jer. xxii. 13.) What else is the practice of South Carolina or Georgia?

"*Behold, the hire of the labourers who have reaped down your fields, which is of you kept back by fraud,*

---

[*] Shaffner, 282.

crieth: and the cries of them that have reaped are entered into the ears of the Lord of sabaoth," (James v. 4.) To whom does God say this if not to the planters of Louisiana and Mississippi?

"*He shall judge the poor of the people, he shall save the children of the needy, and shall break in pieces the oppressor. He shall spare the poor and needy, and shall save the souls of the needy. He shall redeem their soul from deceit and violence: and precious shall their blood be in his sight,*" (Ps. lxxii. 4, 13, 14.)

Mr Lincoln's proclamation could not be more dangerous in the eyes of a planter than these passages, or more likely to stir up a servile war.

Preachers with the fear of the magistrate before their eyes may flatter wicked slave-owners; but God flatters them not: and slaves who read His Word know to what misery He has doomed those who oppress the poor, or shed their blood, or contaminate their wives and their daughters.

While, then, the Word of God brings down the wicked planter, however exalted his position, however large his estates, at the same time it exalts his Christian slaves. For Jesus and His apostles have made the poorest slave who believes, brother to all other believers. "*One is your Master, even Christ; and all ye are brothers,*" (Matt. xxiii. 8.) "*There is neither Greek nor Jew, bond nor free: but Christ is all, and in all,*" (Col. iii. 11.) "*Ye are all the children of God by faith in Christ Jesus,*" (Gal. iii. 26.) "*There is neither Jew nor Greek, there is neither bond nor free; for ye are all one in Christ Jesus,"* (Gal. iii. 28.) The meanest slave in South Carolina who believes in Jesus is represented by the Word of God to be as much superior to the richest planter in the State, who lives in sin, as a child of God is superior to a child of the devil, (John viii. 44; 1 John iii. 8–10; with John i. 12.) All who read with faith the Word of God, learn to despise vice in gems and gold, while they honour godliness in rags. Every Christian will acknowledge a slave in the hoe-gang as a brother, and will warn the richest voluptuary that he is a slave of sin, who will soon have his part in the lake of fire. But these revelations Southerners do not like to dawn on the darkness of their slaves.

Another effect of reading the Word of God is still more inconvenient to the slave-holders. It must enlighten and fortify the conscience. When Nebuchadnezzar bade those young slaves worship his god on pain of being burned alive, they answered, "Our God, whom we serve, is able to deliver us from the furnace; and he will deliver us out of thine hand, O king. But if not, be it known to thee, O king, that we will not serve thy gods, nor worship the golden image which thou hast set up." They feared God more than the imperial slave-holder. They had read the Bible; and they had a conscience which no honours could bribe, and which no threats could terrify. So every South Carolinian slave, believing in Jesus, and acquainted with the Word of God, would on every occasion obey God rather than please a tyrant; any Christian man would rather be cut to pieces himself than torment another innocent man at his master's bidding; any Christian woman, taught by the same book, would rather die than sacrifice her purity to his lusts. So the conscience of his servants would constantly fire up the wrath of the slave-holder, as the conscience of the three Jews kindled the fury of their master. Dr Flint was only Nebuchadnezzar in his way when he thus threatened Linda Brent:—

"'You can do what I require; and if you are faithful to me, you will be as virtuous as my wife.'

'The Bible does not say so.'

'How dare you preach to me about your infernal Bible? I am your master, and you shall obey me.'"[*]

Vicious and violent slave-holders would not like to hear their slaves quote the Word of God against them; and the best way to prevent them from doing so is to hinder them from reading it.

Besides all these influences of the Bible, it would, further, make slaves think. Thought leads to knowledge, and knowledge is power. The planters of South Carolina had a very true instinct when they drove away Mr Tupper, who was beginning to preach to their slaves. "Verbal instruction," they said, "will increase the desire of the black population to learn. We thus expect that a system of improvement will follow from the force of circumstances which will ultimately revolutionise our civil institutions."[†]

Religious knowledge leads to secular knowledge.

[*] Linda Brent, 115.   [†] Olmsted, ii. 214.

Slaves permitted to read the Bible would soon read Helper, Olmsted, "Uncle Tom's Cabin," "News from the North," &c., and it would be impossible long to retain them in bondage. Some of them, doubtless, now do so. These are like that one whom his owner described to Mr Olmsted in the following terms:—

"I bought him because he was a first-rate nigger; and I thought I could break him off running away. I expect he is making for Mexico. Night before last, I engaged with a man who has got some first-rate nigger dogs to meet me here to-night. He is a real black nigger, and carried off a double-barrelled gun with him. He is as humble a nigger when he is at work as ever I have seen; but a mighty resolute nigger. No man has more resolution. He is a nigger of sense,—as much sense as a white man."*

Millions, like him, who think and feel as men because they have knowledge and religion, must, in one way or another, get their liberty.

SECTION VIII—EFFECTS OF SLAVERY.

The laws of God are not violated with impunity. The slave-holders, though hitherto they have been most prosperous, have inflicted incalculable evils upon their slaves, upon the "mean whites," upon themselves, upon their wives and children, upon the churches of which they are members, and upon the clergymen by whom they are taught. Of the slaves, I will only repeat, that slavery has robbed them of their money, shackled their

* Olmsted, ii. 7, 8.

minds, rendered them indolent, false, dishonest, and sensual, destroyed their happiness, and kept them from the knowledge of Christ.

But the wrong which has been done to them has punished the wrong-doers too; for by it the Slave States have been impoverished, degraded, and half-ruined. Let the reader weigh the figures published by Mr Helper, and he will wonder that any man of sense can uphold the system for another day.

Free labour cannot co-exist with slave labour; because when the work of the field is carried on under the whip, all manual labour becomes in men's minds the symbol of abject poverty and of slavish subjection. Whatever, therefore, may be the advantages offered to them, freemen, whether from the North or from Europe, will not settle in the Slave States. No man will encounter general contempt if he can help it, nor place himself where his energy would be viewed with jealousy, and his industry be an object of scorn. Vast tracts, therefore, of cheap and excellent land are left unoccupied. Few Southern whites are skilled artisans; and the mineral wealth of the country is almost wholly neglected. Even the coarse cottons and woollens, which form the clothing of the slaves, come from the North. There is little steam-power; the water-power which exists is not used; and men of capital who have attempted to establish factories have abandoned their undertaking in disgust—unable to command their workmen, and exposed to general contempt. The great slave-holders look down upon the trader: and the capitalist, however enlightened or benevolent, finds himself in a society which scorns and shuns him. Similar prejudices discredit all mercantile employment. And although the slave-holders have exported cottons and other staples of late years to the value of more than 200,000,000 dollars, this large trade has been carried on almost exclusively by Northern men. The value of the crops has indeed been great, and the increase of the cotton trade in England and in France has so raised the price of cotton, and so increased its growth, that one Slave State has been added after another for its production.

The Slave-breeding States have sold their labourers at high prices to the extent of 20,000 per annum; Virginia alone has been making eight millions of dollars annually by this sale; and the cotton-growers, who have bought their labourers, have realised large returns. Still it is to be observed that with this extraordinary prosperity, their increase of wealth has been more apparent than real. During all this enlargement, both of territory and of income, they have never been large customers either to us or to any other nation. From the nature of their system, they never can be. They are themselves so small a class that they cannot consume foreign goods to any extent; the "mean whites," without money and without employment, are still poorer customers; and slaves are no customers at all: so that we must never hope to gain much from a Slave Empire. How, then, do they employ the vast incomes which they receive from their cotton, rice, tobacco, and sugar? Planters who are extravagant, having borrowed from the New York capitalists large sums, the interest must be paid out of their incomes; and cultivation by slave labour is very costly. Their slaves, listless and reluctant, cannot be made by any whipping to do as much work as free labourers. They must pay their managers and overseers, their drivers and their slave-hunters; they must maintain the sick and old slaves; and they often lose their labourers by premature death. On the whole, they do not consume much of the productions of Europe, nor accumulate much capital. Then the effect of slavery upon the land is very bad. Little capital, and less science, being applied to its cultivation, it is soon exhausted. Farms in the North, once reclaimed, are brought into permanent cultivation; but cotton plantations are used up and abandoned. Patches of cotton now appear in the midst of wastes which were once under the hoe; so that each Slave State exhibits, not contiguous farms, where field touches field, as in New England, but small cotton-fields, with large contiguous wastes, ending in larger primeval forests. Slave-holders have large estates, but, without hands to cultivate them, or customers to buy them, or capital to employ upon them, or markets for any variety of produce, find much of them nearly worthless. A farm in Pennsylvania is worth five times as much as a neighbouring farm of the same size in Virginia; though the latter may have all the same natural advantages. In the Slave States, manufactures and commerce are despised; minerals lie idle; free labourers and artisans are almost banished; and nothing remaining but land

and slaves, the land itself becomes nearly worthless, because slave labour exhausts the richest parts, and is too costly for the poorer.

Where the white population is so scattered and so poor, all the usual means of civilisation must become scanty too. Roads cannot pay when they must traverse extended wastes; and without roads small proprietors can derive little profit from distant markets. Schools can scarcely be maintained by those who are too few to fill them, too poor to pay for them, and too ignorant to value them. Without schools there can be few readers, and without readers few book-shops or newspapers. Thus the population must remain depressed and impoverished. All this has happened during a great extension of the cotton trade, which may be again reduced. Cotton-growers in other parts of the world are likely soon to divide the profits of the trade with their American rivals; and should the slave system continue, many of the plantations of the slave-holders will be reduced to desolation, if they should lose the monopoly which alone has given them a precarious, and perhaps momentary importance.*

Fertile lands, which, a few years ago, yielded immense crops, are now abandoned to weeds and snakes; Alabama and Georgia are becoming used up like Virginia and South Carolina; already poverty and dilapidation are everywhere visible; and if this has happened during such an extension of trade, that Virginian slaves

* For these results of slavery, see Olmsted, i. 8, 11-13, 111; ii. 232. Helper, 27, 29, 34, 35, 53, 58, 86, 89.

have gone up from 300 dollars to 1000, what will happen when cotton from India and Queensland, from Africa, from Algeria, from the West Indies and Venezuela, dispute the market with them?

While slavery has thus impoverished the whole territory in which it prevails, its effect upon the "mean whites" has been especially disastrous. Since the working-classes are treated as beasts, deprived of all civil rights, driven to their work by the whip, and killed upon the slightest provocation, all labour like theirs appears to the whites as slavish; and a labourer who does their work becomes, in popular estimation, as contemptible as they are. White men, therefore, whatever may be their needs, shrink from all regular labour. They cultivate their patches of ground, hire themselves out for jobs, or work for a few days in harvest; but they will never submit to habitual control. Their lives are therefore irregular and idle. Affluence in the service of an employer seems to them much more degrading than hardship and want with the command of their own time. They will be as little as possible like slaves. The necessary consequence is, that they are poor. Some of them have lands; but of what use are these, when they have no slaves to cultivate them, and no free labour is to be had? It is the prerogative of a white to lounge; and as they will do little for themselves, their lands can do little for them. Properties which in Massachusetts or Connecticut would make them rich, leave them poorer than the Northern labourer who has not an acre of his own. Their houses are rude and ill-furnished; they wear the coarsest clothing; they vegetate rather than live. Squatters round the cotton estates, and dotting at great distances the territory, which comprehends vast forests and abandoned wastes, they can have no literary advantages. Few schoolmasters are attracted to neighbourhoods so unpromising; and these few have the lowest qualifications. Libraries and newspapers are rarely to be found. The hawker seldom carries his literary treasure to a people so sure to starve him by the smallness of their numbers, their want of money, and their disregard of knowledge. Thus their ignorance prolongs itself; and as knowledge is power, so ignorance is impotence. Without industry, without objects in life, without a knowledge of what others are doing, how can they improve? They can fish, hunt, and shoot; they can sharpen a bowie knife, and despise a Yankee because he works like a slave; but they can do nothing else. Apathetic and unenterprising, they live without progress, and leave their children to base and aimless lives like their own.

As industry promotes virtue, so idleness is the parent of crime; and these non-slaveholding whites are in circumstances which especially tempt them. Poor, in contact with wealth, they see great houses which shame the meanness of their sheds; and they touch great estates where gangs of labourers under the whip reap golden harvests for their fortunate neighbours. How they must long for the re-opening of the African slave-trade, which would give them also slaves for almost nothing, who would turn the wilderness near them into mines of gold for them too. Meanwhile, if they cannot grow rich, they can trade a little with the slaves. Slaves from whom their owner has stolen everything think that they may fairly steal a little from him; and the mean whites are at hand to supply them with whisky or other luxuries in return for their stolen goods. The habitual intercourse between these whites and the slave population degrades them to its level. Although the law forbids them to marry coloured women, it takes no notice of a lawless intercouse which only gives to the slaveholder brown children whom he can sell at better prices than the black. Too proud to imitate the industry of the slave, which would enrich and improve them, they are mean enough to debase themselves by the imitation of his vices. Indolence, poverty, ignorance, and vice give them up helpless into the hands of the slave-holders. Theoretically they are freemen who have the privilege of a free country; but in reality they have little political influence; and not unjustly are they termed by Mr Helper, half slaves. According to their numbers, they should exercise the powers of a majority in their States; but the slave-holders have contrived to get all the power into their own hands. From the influence which the wealthy and the educated must ever exercise over the ragged and the ignorant, the slave-holders have always been able to secure in their legislatures and in the Congress at Washington representatives entirely devoted to their interests. In the North, there are different political parties, because men of all classes read and think: in the South, there is but one; not because there are not opposite interests, but because the slave-holders have eyes, and the mean whites have none. The legislation, the executive government, the administration of the law, the taxation, and the command of the militia, are in the hands of the oligarchs; and the mean whites without eyes have to follow where they lead. Under these circumstances, any man of energy among them might be expected to be impatient. Mr Helper became, by the emancipation of his father's slaves, one of these non-slaveholding whites. Possessed of a property which in a Free State would have made him comfortable, but which in a Slave State was almost worthless, he felt keenly, and has pointed out with acrimony, the injury which the mean whites have suffered from the system. A more undesirable existence than theirs is scarcely to be imagined. They are debased by contact with the slaves who are beneath them, and oppressed by the shadow of the slave-holders who are above them. They despise the slave because he is degraded by the whip, and the slave despises them because they are so poor and helpless. They dislike and dread the slave-holder because he is haughty and overbearing; and they are disliked by him in return because they are so coarse and so worthless. At the same time, they are no friends of the North, because, in their untravelled and unreflecting folly, they obtain all their notions of their free countrymen from the slave-holders and their journals. Misled by these, they imagine that the New Englanders work like slaves for a bare existence, and by seeking to emancipate the slaves, wish to make these slaves their equals. So these mean whites are befooled. Poor, yet proud—discontented, yet unwilling to improve their condition—unhappy, yet dreading the changes which would give them happiness, they are the tools employed by the slaveholders to keep the negroes in bondage, to impoverish the country, and to perpetuate their own degradation.*

Slave-holders support this system, because it gives them wealth and power; but they cannot be defended from the charge of selfishness, because they obtain these advantages at the expense of four millions of men and women, whom they rob of their rights, reduce to brutish stupidity, and render utterly miserable. That charge would remain, if they experienced from it no mischief themselves. Every humane man would reject a happiness to be obtained by the tears of others. But almost all writers have agreed that its worst evils descend upon themselves. It renders them imperious, passionate, and cruel; many are tempted by it to become profligate, and some ruffianly. Not a few oppose the religious instruction of the slave, and they have forbidden him by law to read the Word of God. The habits of the poorer class of slave-holders are, according to Mr Olm-

---

* See Olmsted, i., 12, 13, 81, 82, 83, 112, 115, 116, 231, 232, 251, 253, 372; ii., 196, 327, 355, 356. Helper, 29, 35, 40-43, 74, 83, 86, 88, 93, 121, 129, 189, 345, 365, 403, 404. Ludlow, 49, 189, 190.

sted, coarse and repulsive; and the richer, if they are more refined, are at the same time more exposed to the vices engendered by unbridled power.

Overseers, less educated than owners, coming into more frequent collision with the slaves, and urged by their interests to cruelty, are said to be generally bad men. "Is the general character of overseers bad?" said Mr Olmsted to a slave-holder. "They are the curse of this country, sir," answered the proprietor; "the worst men in the community."* "Often," said another, "they are coarse, brutal, and licentious."† That was in Virginia; but, far away in Alabama, another man reported to Mr Olmsted:—"The overseers have always to go about armed; their life would not be safe if they didn't. As it is, they very often get cut pretty bad." "If they make plenty of cotton, the owners never ask how many niggers they kill."‡ One of these men whom Mr Olmsted met wore no waistcoat, but carried a pistol in the pocket of his trousers.§ In the bed-room of a second he found pistols, other arms, ammunition, and handcuffs;‖ and a third said to him, "I wouldn't mind killing a nigger more than I would a dog."¶

Women cannot witness this violence in their husbands and others without catching something of the same spirit. One wife of a slave-holder having related that the mob had seized a negress, and hung her on the spot, said they ought to have piled some wood

* Olmsted, i. 53.   † Ibid., 94.   ‡ Ibid., ii. 185.
§ Ibid., 144.   ‖ Ibid., 175.   ¶ Ibid., 203.

round her, and burned her to death. "We afterwards heard her scolding one of her girls. The girl getting the best of the argument, the mistress told her, that if she said another word, she would have two hundred lashes given her."* Another, wife of an "opulent squire," said to Mr Olmsted, in the presence of a negro woman and two boys, "I wouldn't like to live where niggers was free. I reckon that niggers are the meanest critters on earth,—so mean and nasty!—such vile, saucy things!"†

The mistress of Linda Brent would sit in her chair, and see a woman whipped till the blood trickled from every stroke of the lash.‡ Mrs Wade, another slaveowner, lashed the slaves herself in her barn, till one of her slaves said to Linda Brent, "It's hell in missis' house; day and night I prays to die."§ Another "very religious lady" is mentioned by Mr Olmsted, who, besides extorting from her slaves the most oppressive labours, had them whipped for the most trivial violations of her orders.‖ These ladies may be thought to be unlike the majority in the South. Perhaps they are; but that there are many tainted with the ferocity of their husbands is, I fear, indicated by the following fact:—

"A senator from Massachusetts, Charles Sumner, in a speech of his, called Senator Butler of South Carolina, and Senator Douglas, the Don Quixote and Sancho Panza of slavery. A day or two after, as he was bend-

* Olmsted, ii. 13.   † Ibid., 129.   ‡ Linda Brent, 22.
§ Ibid., 74.   ‖ Olmsted, ii. 100.

ing over his desk, Mr Brooks, a relative of Mr Butler, came behind, and struck him repeatedly over the head with, I believe, a heavy cane. Mr Sumner remained laid up for months from the effects of this outrage, which seemed at one time as if it would deprive him of his reason. Incredible to say, this brutal assailant of a stooping man leaped at one bound into the position of a Southern hero. Although expelled by the House of Representatives, he was immediately sent back to it. Addresses and eulogies were showered upon him, and the ladies of South Carolina presented him with a cane as an emblem of his prowess."* "In the South, his name is never yet mentioned without the term gallant or courageous, spirited or noble, is attached to it. The man who has been accustomed from his childhood to see men beaten when they have no chance to defend themselves—to see other men whip women without interference, remonstrance, or any expression of indignation, must have a certain quality, which is an essential part of personal honour, blunted, if not destroyed. The quality which we detest in the assassination of an enemy is essentially constant in all slavery."† The ladies of South Carolina and of New Orleans have not escaped it. One of these Southern ladies, lately, at New Orleans, as she saw the coffin of a brave and gentle youth pass her door, whose only fault had been that he had been an officer in the service of his country, laughed and mocked aloud, and spat upon his coffin in contempt.

* Ludlow, 259. † Olmsted, ii. 349.

Of these Southerners, the Special Correspondent of the *Times* says, "The intensity of hate flushes the cheek and clenches the teeth. . . . . If anything, the exuberance of animosity is more perceptible in the flashing eyes and eager earnestness of the women. . . . . It seems generally conceded, that General Butler has converted the sons of Louisiana mothers into demons of more than earthly ferocity."* But, says Mr Ward Beecher, "Southern men have been tame and cool in comparison with the fury of Southern women."† If the men of New Orleans are indeed "demons of more than earthly ferocity," and yet are "tame and cool" in comparison with the New Orleans women, what must these be? Perhaps hatred

> "Has fill'd them, from the crown to the toe, top-full
> Of direst cruelty; made thick their blood;
> Stopp'd up th' access and passage of remorse,
> That no compunctious visitings of nature
> Shake their fell purpose;"

and when they see the "demons of more than earthly ferocity" growing tame from seeing that the rebellion is both a sin and a blunder, they may remind each her husband or her son of his oath to the Confederate Government, which, like every sinful oath, has no force, in terms like these:—

> "I have given suck, and know
> How tender 'tis to love the babe that milks me.
> I would, while it was smiling in my face,
> Have pluck'd my nipple from his boneless gums,
> And dash'd the brains out, had I but so sworn
> As you have done to this."

---

* *Times*, Nov. 4.   † *New York Independent*, Oct. 9.

When some such ladies insulted the soldiers of General Butler, he directed them to treat the insults of these ladies as they would those of loose women in the streets; that is, with silent pity. For this he has been incessantly vilified by men who perhaps, in the sight of God, are not either so pure or so kind-hearted as he is. It is a pleasure and a duty to treat women with respect and gentleness; and no nation does it so much as the people of the United States. But when women will unsex themselves, will indulge more than the fierceness of man, will thirst for blood and exult in brutal assaults like that of Brooks, they cannot look for the language of courtesy.

The effect of this system upon children must necessarily be deplorable. Licentiousness and cruelty are the two great sins of the South; and children soon catch these from their elders. If a Virginia or South Carolina boy associates with depraved slaves, he will become licentious; and if he sees his father passionate, cruel, and ruffianly, he will soon be as bad or worse. Here I will again let American authorities speak:—

"There must doubtless be an unhappy influence on the manners of our people produced by the existence of slavery among us. The whole commerce between master and slave is a perpetual exercise of the most boisterous passions. Our children see this, and learn to imitate it. The parent storms, the child looks on, puts on the same airs in the circle of smaller slaves, gives a loose rein to the worst of passions; and thus nursed, educated, and daily exercised in tyranny, cannot but be stamped by it with odious peculiarities. The man must be a prodigy who can retain his manners and his morals under such circumstances."*

"People that own niggers are always mad with them about something; half their time is spent in swearing and yelling at them." †

"Children are fond of the company of negroes. If in this association the child becomes familiar with lascivious manners and conversation, an impression is made which lasts perhaps for life. Many young men and women, who have made shipwreck of all their earthly hopes, have been led to the fatal step by the seeds of corruption which, in the days of their childhood and youth, were sown in their hearts by the lascivious manners of their father's negroes." ‡

"I've got as good niggers as anybody. They will lie and steal; but lying and stealing are not the worst of it. I've got a family of children; and I don't like to have such degraded beings round my house while they are growing up. I know what the consequences are to children of growing up among slaves." §

"I never conversed," says Mr Olmsted, "with a cultivated Southerner on the effects of slavery that he did not express a wish to have his children educated where they should be free from demoralising association with slaves. That this association is almost

* Jefferson, in Helper, 153.
† Alabama Gentleman to Mr Olmsted, ii. 135.
‡ *Southern Cultivator;* Olmsted, i. 222.
§ Alabama Slaveholder; Olmsted, ii. 97.

inevitably corrupting is very generally admitted." *
Mr Olmsted gives painful instances of the profligacy of Southern youths, which I shall pass by, and shall only give one or two instances of their violence:—

"We stopped one night at the house of a planter. This gentleman had thirty or forty negroes, and two legitimate sons. One was an idle young man; the other was, at eight years old, a swearing, tobacco-chewing bully and ruffian. We heard him whipping a puppy behind the house, his father and mother being at hand. His language was an evident imitation of his father's mode of dealing with his slaves. 'I've got an account to settle with you. I've let you go about long enough. I'll teach you who's your master. There, go now, God damn you; but I haven't got through with you yet.' 'You stop that cursing,' said his father. 'What do *you* do when you get mad? reckon you cuss some; so now you'd better shut up.'" †

"I have seen a girl, twelve years old, stop an old man on the public road, demand to know where he was going, order him to return to the plantation, and enforce her command by threatening that she would have him well whipped if he did not instantly obey." ‡

When a boy of fifteen, evidently the son of the proprietor, saw a poor girl flogged, who writhed and screamed in her agony, as the overseer lashed her naked stomach, "the boy," says Mr Olmsted, "evidently had not the slightest sympathy with my emotion." §

* Olmsted, ii. 230. † Ibid., 9, 10.
‡ Ibid., 351. § Ibid., 206.

"Two sons of Mr Payne were shooting pigeons on the plantation of Mr Mays, (near Lynchburg,) and went to the tobacco-house, where the overseer and hands were housing tobacco. One of the boys had a string of pigeons, and the other had none. A negro asked the boy who had no pigeons, 'Where his were?' He replied, 'he had killed none, but could kill him,' and fired. The load took effect in the head, and caused death in a few hours." *

"Two young men were intimate friends, till one of them, taking offence at some foolish words uttered by the other, challenged him. A large crowd assembled to see the duel. The combatants came armed with rifles; and at the first interchange of shots, the challenged man fell, disabled by a ball in the thigh. The other, throwing down his rifle, walked towards him, and, kneeling by his side, drew a bowie-knife and deliberately butchered him. The crowd permitted this. The execrable assassin still lives in the community, has since married, and, as far as my informant could judge, his social position has been rather advanced than otherwise from his thus dealing with his enemy."

"How can men retain true manhood who daily see men beaten whose position renders resistance impracticable, and not only men but women too?" †

It is a lamentable fact that this system vitiates even the religion of the South. "The necessity of accepting and apologising for the exceedingly low morality of

* Olmsted, ii. 191. † Ibid., 231.

the nominally religious slaves, together with the familiarity with this immorality which all classes acquire, renders the existence of a very elevated standard of morals among the whites almost an impossibility." *

Linda Brent's testimony is as follows:—"There is a great difference between Christianity and religion at the South. If a man goes to the communion-table, and pays money into the treasury of the church, he is called religious. If a pastor has offspring by a woman not his wife, if she is coloured, it does not hinder his continuing to be their shepherd." "Southern women often marry a man, knowing that he is the father of many slaves. They do not trouble themselves about it." "This bad institution deadens the moral sense, even in white women, to a fearful extent." †

Perhaps the instances in which a pastor and his people despise the law of God in the manner mentioned above by Linda Brent may be rare; but in the other matter of cruelty, I fear the ministers have not escaped the prevailing temper of the slaveholders; at least, the few of which I have heard or read appear to have been infected. Mr Terry, a Presbyterian minister, in Troop county, Alabama, flogged a slave to death one Sunday morning before preaching to his congregation, and was never troubled about it.

Mr Dorson, a Baptist minister at Columbus, Georgia, sold in June last his two grandchildren, and their mother, Caroline Martin, who had lived with his son, to her brother, Mr Sella Martin; but he would not

* Olmsted, ii. 229. † Linda Brent, 115, 57.

let them go till he had got for them 2000 dollars,—a very high price in the present state of the slave market.*

In the year 1860, a poor slave was executed in Alabama for having struck his master on the head, as Mr Brooks struck Mr Sumner. The only difference in the two cases was that the cane of Mr Brooks was lighter than the bludgeon of the slave, and that, while Mr Brooks by several blows stunned the one man, the slave by one blow killed the other. For the one assault, which was made with almost no provocation, the South made Mr Brooks a hero; for the other, which was probably accomplished in the madness to which insufferable wrongs may goad even the most patient, the Southerners roasted the slave to death at a slow fire, and clergymen were there to consecrate the brutal act by their approval.†

I have already mentioned that near Knoxville, Tennessee, when a negro was publicly burned alive, a Methodist preacher wrote, "The punishment was unequal to the crime. Had we been there, we should have taken a part, and even suggested the pinching of pieces out of him with red-hot pincers, the cutting off of a limb at a time, and then burning them all in a heap."‡

Bishop Polk, of Louisiana, may be less sanguinary than that Wesleyan, but not, I think, less culpable.

---

* See Life of Sella Martin, further on.
† Olmsted, ii. 348.   ‡ Ibid., ii. 351, 352.

Not content with preaching up the rebellion, he took arms to support it. Leaving his clergy to themselves, and his four hundred negroes to the overseers, he became a general of division, exchanged his lawn for epaulettes, and joined General Beauregard at Corinth. Within the entrenchments of that stronghold he might in turn write pastorals to his clergy, orders to his overseers, and directions to his brigadiers and colonels. Not to serve his government, but to defy it,—not to defend his country, but to dismember and ruin it,—he led on his troops to the slaughter of their countrymen at Shiloh; determined, like his brother slaveholders, to perpetuate slavery or perish.

Finally, Mr Palmer, of New Orleans, animated with a zeal for the enslavement of his fellow-men, scarcely less martial than that of Bishop Polk, has written thus :—" This argument . . . establishes the solemnity of our present trust TO PRESERVE AND TRANSMIT OUR EXISTING SYSTEM OF DOMESTIC SERVITUDE, WITH THE RIGHT UNCHANGED BY MAN, TO GO AND ROOT ITSELF WHEREVER PROVIDENCE AND NATURE MAY CARRY IT. This charge we will discharge in the face of the worst possible peril. Not till the last man has fallen behind the last rampart shall it drop from our hands.

" We may, if we succumb, for a generation enjoy comparative ease, and die in peace; but our children will go forth beggared from the homes of their fathers. Sapped, circumvented, undermined, the institutions of your soil will be overthrown, and within five-and-twenty years the history of St Domingo will be the record of Louisiana. If dead men's bones can tremble, ours will move under the muttered curses of sons and daughters, denouncing the blindness and the love of ease which have left them an inheritance of woe." *

SECTION IX.—NARRATIVE OF THE REV. JOHN SELLA MARTIN.

John Sella Martin was born at Charlotte, North Carolina. His father is now agent of the railroad which has its terminus at that place. His mother was the property of Mrs Henderson of Charlotte, who was his father's aunt. I have lately read a letter from his father to him at Boston, signed, "Your affectionate father;" yet, this father, according to Southern custom, left him in bondage; and still leaves his daughter and her two children to suffer all the horrors of slavery. One night, while they were living in peace at Charlotte, Sella's mother returning from a visit to a friend found a man in her cottage who sternly bade her take off her finery and follow him. To complain was useless, to resist impossible. Mrs Henderson had sold her and her children, and the trader was now come in the dead of night to carry them off. While Mrs Henderson was counting the money which she had obtained by selling her nephew and niece to a

* Palmer: "Slavery a Divine Trust," &c., pp. 12, 19.

brute, and while Mr Martin slept comfortably on his bed of down, his two children and the woman whom he had wronged were forced from their home, and were hurried to the place where the trader had penned his human cattle. What tears and groans, what curses and stripes mingled in the pen that night, Sella was too young to remember; nor could he know what happened to the other victims of slave-holding greed. But he and his mother were sold to Dr Chipley, who then lived at Columbus, Georgia, and who now lives at Lexington in Kentucky. When Sella was about nine years old, he was taken for a debt by Mr Edward E. Powers. He was thus separated from his mother; but could visit her sometimes, as she was living in the same place. Mr Powers used to have his meals at a hotel, and not wanting Sella at his house, made an arrangement with the landlord that Sella should wait at table, and in return for his board and lodging should go on errands for the landlord. At this time Mr Powers placed him at a Sunday-school. Here, as Sella recollects, he was often taught that slaves should obey their masters, (Col. iii. 22, 1 Pet. ii. 18;) but never that slaves as well as freemen are children of God by faith in Jesus, and as dear to God as the Christian whose skin is white, (Gal. iii. 26–28.) Slave-holders can misapply Scripture to suit their purposes, as Satan did to Jesus, (Matt. iv.) In that school no scholar was taught to read, for, by a law of the State, any white who teaches a slave to read is liable to a fine of $500. But the tyranny of that unrighteous law the poor friendless boy contrived to evade.

During this part of his life he often played at marbles with white boys; and, being expert in the game, won many. Of those he made excellent use, by carrying a spelling-book in his pocket, and by giving a certain number of marbles to any boy for teaching him a word of spelling. The bribe conquered their fear of parental injunctions; so, thus, word after word was lodged in his memory. By degrees he learned to read, and excited the admiration of his fellow-slaves by reading for them scraps of the newspaper. While he was so exercising his power of reading, he was often asked by the negroes to write for them. His marbles furnished him with the means of learning; for his spelling-book having been replaced by a black board and a piece of chalk, he used to tell his playmates that he would give so many marbles to any boy who could write a better letter than he. Accepting his challenge, they would write letters on his board; and he, after observing how they formed the letters, would pay them the marbles, acknowledging that he could not write so well as they had done. These letters were afterwards practised in secret; and at length the power of writing was added to that of reading.

When he went one day to see his mother at Dr Chipley's, he found that she had been sent, in exchange for another slave, to Mr Terry, a Presbyterian minister, who had a plantation in Troop county, Alabama; and that his sister had been sold to Mr Young, in Columbus. After four years of absence, becoming impatient beyond endurance, because Mr Powers, who had often promised to let him see his mother, never fulfilled that promise, he forged a pass, and walked sixty miles to see her. She was almost his only friend. But the joy of their meeting had not lasted many minutes, when she remembered the danger to which his filial affection had exposed him. That night he rested in her cottage, but before dawn the next morning, he sought shelter in a neighbouring wood. It was Sunday: and that afternoon, as he lay in his concealment, he observed some negroes enter the wood, dig a hole near him, and throw into it a dead body. Night enabled him to return to his mother; who, in answer to his questions, gave him the following explanation of the wood scene. A slave who had been bought by Mr Terry had that morning refused to be flogged, whereupon he was seized, his hands were tied, and he was raised by a rope which passed over a beam in the smoke-house till his feet just touched the ground. Mr Terry then gave him four hundred lashes with a zeal so worthy a slaveholder that some of the negroes said, "He is dead." At which announcement Mr Terry gave him seven more lashes, and then exclaiming, "He is dead, is he? let us see," opened his knife, and stuck it into the dead man's foot. He had done his work. Had he cut out his victim's eyes, or put a slow fire under him, it would have been in vain; but the slave was gone where the slave-holder's fury could not reach him. Not so the shuddering negroes who had aided in the murder. "Take warning," said the murderer; "that is what you shall have if you resist me." Such was his sermon in the smoke-house. What his text was in the church, to which he immediately rode off, Sella does not know; but he preached, as Sella afterwards heard, on the wickedness of negroes, assuring his congregation that one of his had died that morning of passion. The only effect of that murder was, that the whole congregation pitied the poor minister who was plagued by so perverse a slave. Witnesses of the murder were there; but how could they speak? The law allows no slave to give evidence against a white man; and each would have too keen a recollection of the smoke-house ever to utter a word, except among each other. I know not whether Mr Terry is still alive, but alive or dead he cannot escape the eye or hand of God; and if he still lives to flog other slaves to death, perhaps when he reads the Word of God, he will meet with this passage, "Murderers shall have their part in the lake which burneth with fire and brimstone."

That evening, while Sella was with his mother, a step was heard at the door of the cottage. "Hide! hide!" said the frightened woman. Scarcely was he shut in her wardrobe when Mr Terry entered. "Where is your son?" She was silent. "Where is your son?" Although she saw the fury in his face, and learned it by the thunder of his voice, she would not betray her boy. A blow from his stick then laid her forehead open, and she fell bleeding to the ground. Sella, who through a chink saw all, could not bear it; and springing out, threw Mr Terry down, and then knelt down to help his mother. The reverend slave-holder, seeing his advantage, stunned him by blows upon his head. For hours he lay insensible; and, when his senses returned, he found himself bound hand and foot, with a negro standing over him. Almost the first sounds which came upon his ear were those of heavy blows in the smoke-house. "Where is my mother?" "In the smoke-house." Mr Terry had been flogging her a quarter of an hour. "Oh, let me see her! Do, do!" As the only answer to his prayer, he was carried bound to the waggon, which Mr Powers had sent for him from Columbus, and in that city was thrown into prison.

By the aid of some other negro prisoners he escaped with them to the woods; but after various adventures was caught, and carried back to prison, where he remained nine months.

Here his chief companion was a Boston man, named Green, confined for theft, from whom he learned much respecting the geography of the country, the difference between the North and the South, and the way in which he might escape: indeed, far more than a slave shut out by law from all instruction could hope to learn anywhere but in prison. At the end of nine months he returned to live with Mr Powers.

Meanwhile, his sister Caroline had been sold by Mr Young to Mr Dorson, a Baptist minister at Columbus. Nathaniel, his son, using the irresistible power which belonged to him as the son of the owner, constrained her to live with him; and at his death, left her, with his two children, Ada and Charles, slaves to his father. Shortly after, Mr Powers died, and by his will gave freedom to Sella; but the heir set aside the will by some quibble, so that Sella, instead of getting his right, found that he was to be sold by auction to the highest bidder. He was bought by Horace King, a coloured man; but having resisted when this man attempted to flog him, was soon sold by him to a trader. In the service of this trader, with whom he travelled seven months, he became familiar with the horrors of the slave pen.

In the hands of the trader, who buys Christian men and women like cattle, to be sold by him to any savage who will give his price, they are herded together as cattle. The best are crowded with the worst, the most instructed with the most brutalised. If any weep, the trader, who fears that their tears will injure their sale, cries out, "Dry up!" enforcing his command by a blow on the face. They must do all that he bids. The old must say they are young, the weak that they are strong; or they will have the whip; for their price depends upon their age and strength. If a girl can neither cook, nor wash, nor sew, he will force her, by the threat of a flogging, to say that she can do all these; because that increases her value. One girl of colour there, who was gentle, pure, acquainted with the Word of God, and evidently a Christian, taught Sella much gospel truth; yet she was forced to lie, because, had she refused, she would have been laid down on the ground naked before all in the place, and would have been flogged. She was a mulatto Christian, with a sweet countenance, whom the trader would sell to any brute for any purpose. This brute might torture her to any extent which he pleased, if she did not comply with all his wishes. Men calling themselves Christians gave him this power over a defenceless Christian girl; and ministers calling themselves Christians write books to uphold the system which allows it.

Sella himself was sold to Mr Marriott of Carolton, Pickens county, in Alabama. By this man he was allowed to visit his mother, who had been bought by a man named Mangam, and was now living at Columbus, Georgia. Ten days after his arrival she died in faith, expressing her hope in Christ. After his return to Carolton, Mr Marriott sent him to Columbus, Mississippi, where he learnt the trade of a hair-dresser. Through his skill in this art he was able to pay his master fifteen dollars a-month, by practising it on board a steam-boat upon the Alabama River. At the death of his master, who fell a sacrifice to drink, he was again sold by auction. Mr Sherod of Pickensville, who was the highest bidder, instead of being content, as Mr Marriott had been, with fifteen dollars a-month, required him to pay six pounds. Sella was now so much alone in the steam-boat, and went with it so far from home, that Mr Sherod began to think that he would run away. This, which was in itself not improbable, became more likely from the large sum which he had to pay monthly, which he could keep for himself if he could escape.

Troubled by these suspicions, Sherod sold him to Mr Garnett of Mobile, by whom he was taken to New Orleans, and there became hair-dresser on one of the Mississippi steam-boats.

Mr Garnett, in his turn, perhaps under the influence of similar fears, sold him to Mr Cady, a wine merchant at New Orleans, from whom he finally escaped by false papers to Chicago.

There he was safe; for although Mr Cady met him one day in the street, he was afraid to claim him, although the Fugitive Slave Law would have obliged the magistrate to give him up. The anti-slavery feeling in Illinois was so strong, that the slave-holder trembled rather than the slave; and Mr Martin did not even flee.

From that time, he began to deliver anti-slavery lectures. His knowledge increased rapidly. The faith in Christ which, as he thinks, he obtained through the instrumentality of his sister, ripened into decided piety; and he was several times asked to preach. Circumstances now led him to Boston, where he preached to several white congregations, by two of which he was invited to become their minister. Thinking, however, that his negro brethren required his guidance, while white churches could easily obtain ministers, he accepted the call of a black church, and is now their pastor. It was only in the year 1856 that he escaped; but he has so well improved the interval, that he now speaks and preaches as a man of education. His abilities, amiable manners, and Christian temper, so commended him to various friends in this country, that he obtained a sufficient sum to buy the freedom of his sister and her two children. When he last saw her, she said, "If ever you are free, you will try to free us: free Ada first, then Charles; and if you can't do more, I will remain a slave." Mr Dorson, who, though he is a Baptist minister, held his own grandchildren in slavery, would not give them up except at the full market price. Ada is pretty; and if Sella had not bought her, any brute might. She might have been flogged as her grandmother was; or forced against her will into an alliance in which she could not claim the name of wife, as her mother had been. She already suffered much; and she might at any time have been sold in spite or jealousy. But Mr Martin carried back with him the sum demanded by the slave-trading minister who sells his own grandchildren, and they are now safe.

After long anxiety through not obtaining answers to his letters, he received a letter from Mr John Dorson, dated Columbus, Georgia, June 5, (1862,) in which he says, "I received your letter bearing date, Boston, April 9, but did not reply because I saw no way of responding to your proposal, without bringing them to St Louis, or entrusting the business to an agent. I could not do the first, because such madmen and creators of sedition as you and Wendell Phillips had plunged the country into civil war; and I had no disposition to do the last. . . . . The city from which you write, and I suppose where you live, has always been known as the den of social monsters and abolition infidels; and as I know Caroline to be a Christian, I have feared that God would hold me responsible for assisting to plunge her into social and moral ruin."

The hope, however, of obtaining for his son's wife and for her grandchildren 2000 dollars overcame his scruples, and one day Mr Sella Martin received the following note from two Kentucky slave-dealers, Gault and Ketchum:—"While in Columbus, Georgia, the Rev. John Dorson informed us that you had made him an offer for certain slaves in his possession—namely, Caroline and her children, a girl and a boy. He further stated that you had the gold to pay his price of redemption. Upon the strength of his recommendation we bought the slaves. We could easily realise for the girl, who is about sixteen, almost as much as we shall ask you for all; but, as we promised Mr Dorson to let you know that we have them, we write to you to redeem our promise." With fresh anxiety, but with awakened hope, Mr Martin arranged for his journey of six hundred and fifty miles to Cincinnati, and, as he was as much afraid of going into a Slave State as Gault and Ketchum were afraid to bring their slaves into a Free State, he had recourse to an old friend and the ambrotypes. Meantime his sister was taking a journey of four hundred and fifty miles, with slave-dealers and through military posts, but—to a faithful brother and freedom! His letter explains the rest :—

"BOSTON, UNITED STATES, *Sept.* 6.

"MY VERY DEAR FRIEND,—I got back last Friday from Cincinnati after a most successful trip of about eight days. I had written to T. J. Martin, Esq., who was one of my earliest and most faithful friends, asking him to act as my agent in buying my sister and her children, as he had promised to take them into his employ, and he very kindly consented to do so. I wrote to him, also, should he get to Cincinnati before me, to go over to Covington, a place opposite Cincinnati, on the Kentucky side of the river, to where the traders brought my relatives, and get their ambrotypes, so that I should not be cheated in buying others than my sister and the children. He did so, and when I got them, finding by the likenesses that those were the ones I wanted, there was nothing left me to do but to count him out two thousand dollars in gold, and he went over to Covington and made the purchase. The day before when he was over he had tried to get them for less, but he found that it was impossible to do so, and so he was compelled to pay about £412 for them. He was gone about four hours—the time seemed an age to me. A thousand suspicions crept into my mind, and I was depressed by a thousand fears. But had I calculated the time it would take them to make out the papers and get ready to send my sister to the boat, I need not have lived an age of anxiety in four hours.

"When the boat was about three rods from the ferry-landing on this side, Caroline recognised me in the crowd, and came forward on the boat and waved her handkerchief. I soon recognised her, and I suppose behaved myself rather childishly, judging from the description which my friends give me of my actions and utterances. In a few moments more my sister was in my arms. Oh! it was a glorious meeting. My first feelings of joy in gaining my own freedom were not half so ecstatic. . . . .

"My sister brought me some of the soil from my mother's grave, and a piece of the rude board that marks her resting-place. The board is very much decayed, but I shall cherish it with a sacred affection until I shall be permitted to stand near it and hear the song of the slaves' emancipation sung as the jubilee of the race." . . . .

Upon this case the *Daily News* remarks:—
"Enabled by the kindness of his English friends to pay down the market value of his sister and her children, Mr Martin, himself an escaped slave, set about their deliverance from a situation full of horrible contingencies, and addressed himself by letter to their reverend owner. The proposition was, in fact, to buy old Mr Dorson's grandchildren and their mother; but this was not the reverend gentleman's difficulty; he had no delicacy on that score. In fact, as far as getting rid of his unhappy relatives, and obtaining hard cash for them goes, he appears to have acted with con-

siderable decision and promptitude. He shewed the letter to a couple of Kentucky slave-dealers who were in those parts, and these men, seeing an opportunity of making a profit by the transaction, bought them in order to sell them again to Mr Martin. Mr Curwen publishes their letter, which is a fair, straightforward, business-like communication, very different from that which the Rev. Mr Dorson addressed to his anxious correspondent. That reverend gentleman, we are told, is 'greatly respected in his neighbourhood,'—that is, by his fellow slave-owners,—and we can well believe it. If his sermons are like his letters, his function must be to wrest and pervert the principles of our holy religion, and make it the prop and stay of the greatest of social villanies. Such a man must be invaluable in slave society. But there was no reason why he should export his sophistications to Boston. He writes, however, a letter which reminds us of nothing so much as the letters of Taylor, the murderer, lately published. There is in them the same mixture of wickedness and complacent religious sentiment, presuming even to be didactic. . . . .

"Knowing Caroline to be a Christian, he wants to keep her in the slavery which has defiled her, and fears that if he were to sell her into freedom he should be responsible for her moral and social ruin. We wonder what constitutes a woman's ruin down South. However, the reverend gentleman's scruples were not insurmountable, for at the sight of the gold he was ready to entrust not only Caroline, but with her 'the slave girl

Ada, a quadroon, with hazel eyes, aged 16,' to the tender mercies of two travelling speculative slave-dealers, who could have sold them next day to the highest bidder.

"We have not brought forward the case of this hardened and conscience-seared old clergyman for its singularity; for all who know Southern literature or Southern society know that his thoughts and words are such as, under similar circumstances, would be heard wherever slaves have long been held. But we see from this case how helpless the South is to reform itself."*

"If the South is full of such men, what has England to do with the South?"†

SECTION X.—LIFE OF JOSIAH HENSON.

"I was born, June 15, 1789, in Charles county, Maryland, on a farm belonging to Mr Francis Newman, about a mile from Fort Tobacco. My mother was the property of Dr Josiah M'Pherson, but was hired by Mr Newman, to whom my father belonged. The first sorrowful incident I can remember, and it is one which will never be effaced from my recollection, occurred while my mother continued on N.'s farm. One day, the overseer of the plantation attempted a most brutal assault on my mother, of which she informed her husband; and on the same treatment being repeated on a subsequent occasion, my father was so enraged that he severely beat the overseer, and it was only on the intercession of my mother, coupled with

* *Daily News*, Sept. 26, 1862. † Mr Curwen, ibid.

the promise of the overseer that nothing should be said about the transaction, and no proceedings taken against my father, that he refrained from taking his life. This, under the law of the State, was a most serious crime on the part of a slave, and was always visited with severe punishment. The overseer, on recovering from the chastisement my father had inflicted on him, although he had promised to the contrary, immediately proceeded to bring my father to trial, and he was accordingly sentenced to receive one hundred lashes, and to have his right ear cut off. This was carried into effect, notwithstanding the provocation under which the crime was committed; and I well remember the appearance of my father after the punishment, his head being covered with blood, and his back severely lacerated. Furious at such treatment, my father became a different man, and was so morose, disobedient, and intractable, that Mr Newman determined to sell him. He accordingly parted with him, not long after, to his son, who lived in Alabama; and neither my mother nor I ever heard of him again. He was naturally, as I understood afterwards from my mother and other persons, a man of amiable temper, and of considerable energy of character; but it is not strange that he should be essentially changed by such cruelty and injustice under the sanction of the law.

"After the sale of my father, and his leaving Maryland for Alabama, Dr M'Pherson would no longer hire out my mother. She returned, therefore, to the estate of the doctor. My mother, and her young family of three girls and three boys, of which I was the youngest, resided on this estate for two or three years, during which my only recollections are of being rather a pet of the doctor's, who thought I was a bright child, and of being much impressed with what I afterwards recognised as the deep piety and devotional feeling and habits of my mother. I do not know how or where she acquired her knowledge of God, or her acquaintance with the Lord's Prayer, which she so frequently repeated and taught me to repeat. I remember seeing her often on her knees.

"After this brief period of comparative comfort, however, the death of Dr M'Pherson brought about a revolution in our condition. The doctor was riding from one of his scenes of riotous excess, when, falling from his horse, in crossing a little run, not a foot deep, he was unable to save himself from drowning.

"In consequence of his decease, it became necessary to sell the estate and the slaves, in order to divide the property among the heirs; and we were all put up at auction and sold to the highest bidder, and scattered over various parts of the country. My brothers and sisters were bid off one by one, while my mother, holding my hand, looked on in an agony of grief, the cause of which I but ill understood at first, but which dawned on my mind with dreadful clearness as the sale proceeded. My mother was then separated from me, and put up in her turn. She was bought by a man named Isaac Riley, residing in Montgomery county, and then I was offered to the assembled purchasers. My mother, half distracted with parting for ever from all her children, pushed through the crowd, while the bidding for me was going on, to the spot where her new master was standing. She fell at his feet, and clung to his knees, entreating him, in tones that a mother only could command, to buy her *baby* as well as herself, and spare to her one of her little ones at least. Will it, can it be believed that this man, thus appealed to, was capable not merely of turning a deaf ear to her supplication, but of disengaging himself from her with such violent blows and kicks, as to reduce her to the necessity of creeping out of his reach, and mingling the groan of bodily suffering with the sob of a breaking heart? I was bought by a stranger. Almost immediately, however, whether my childish strength, at five or six years of age, was overmastered by such scenes and experiences, or from some accidental cause, I fell sick, and seemed to my new master so little likely to recover, that he proposed to Riley, the purchaser of my mother, to take me, too, at such a trifling rate, that it could not be refused. I was thus providentially restored to my mother.

"The character of Riley, the master whom I faithfully served for many years, is by no means an uncommon one in any part of the world. Coarse and vulgar in his habits, unprincipled and cruel in his general deportment, and especially addicted to the vice of licentiousness, his slaves had little opportunity for relaxation from wearying labour, were supplied with the scantiest means of sustaining their toil by necessary food, and had no security for personal rights. The natural tendency of slavery is to convert the master into a tyrant, and the slave into the cringing, treacherous, false, and thieving victim of tyranny. Riley and his slaves were no exception to the general rule, but might be cited as apt illustrations of the nature of the case.

"The principal food of those upon my master's plantation consisted of corn meal and salt herrings; to which was added in summer, a little buttermilk, and a few vegetables, which each might raise for himself and his family, on the little piece of ground which was assigned to him for the purpose, called a truck patch. The meals were two daily. The first, or breakfast, was taken at twelve o'clock, after labouring from daylight; and the other when the work of the remainder of the day was over. The only dress was of tow cloth, which for the young, and often even for those who had passed the period of childhood, consisted of a single garment, something like a shirt, but longer, reaching to the ankles; and for the older, a pair of pantaloons, or a gown, according to the sex; while some kind of round jacket, or overcoat, might be added in winter, a wool hat once in two or three years, for the males, and a pair of coarse shoes once a year. Our lodging was in log huts, of a single small room, with no other floor than the trodden earth, in which ten or a dozen persons —men, women, and children—might sleep, but which could not protect them from dampness and cold, nor permit the existence of the common decencies of life. There were neither beds nor furniture of any description—a blanket being the only addition to the dress of the day, for protection from the chillness of the air or the earth. In these hovels were we penned at night, and fed by day; here were the children born, and the sick—neglected. Such were the provisions for the daily toil of the slave.

"The condition of the male slave is bad enough, Heaven knows; but that of the female, compelled to perform unfit labour, sick, suffering, and bearing the burdens of her own sex unpitied and unaided, as well as the toils which belong to the other, has often oppressed me with a load of sympathy.

"By the detection of the knavery of the overseer, who plundered his employer, and through my watchfulness was caught in the act and dismissed, I was promoted to be superintendent of the farm work, and managed to raise more than double the crops, with more cheerful and willing labour than was ever seen on the estate before.

"Previous to my attaining this important station, however, an incident occurred. There was a person living at Georgetown, a few miles only from Riley's plantation, whose business was that of a baker, and whose character was that of an upright, benevolent, Christian man. This man occasionally served as a minister of the gospel, and preached in a neighbourhood where preachers were somewhat rare at that period. One Sunday, when he was to officiate in this way, at a place three or four miles distant, my mother persuaded me to ask master's leave to go and hear him; and although such permission was not given freely or often, yet his favour to me was shewn for this once, by allowing me to go. Up to this period of my life, and I was then eighteen years old, I had never heard a sermon, nor any discourse or conversation whatever upon religious topics, except what had been impressed upon me by my mother, of the responsibility of all to a Supreme Being. When I arrived at the place of meeting, the services were so far advanced that the speaker was just beginning his discourse, from the text, Heb. ii. 9: 'That he, by the grace of God, should taste death for every man.' This was the first text of the Bible to which I had ever listened, knowing it to be such. I was wonderfully impressed with the use which the preacher made of the last words of the text, *for every man.* He said, the death of Christ was not designed for the benefit of a select few only, but for the salvation of the world, for the bond as well as the free; and he dwelt on the glad tidings of the gospel to the poor, the persecuted, and the distressed, its deliverance to the captive, and the liberty wherewith Christ has made us free, till my heart burned within me, and I was in a state of the greatest excitement at the thought that such a being as Jesus Christ had been described should have died for me— for *me* among the rest—a poor, despised, abused slave, who was thought by his fellow-creatures fit for nothing but unrequited toil and ignorance, for mental and bodily degradation. I immediately determined to find out something more about Christ, and revolving the things which I had heard in my mind as I went home, I became so excited that I turned aside from the road into the woods, and prayed to God for light and for aid with an earnestness, which, however unenlightened, was at least sincere and heartfelt; and which the subsequent course of my life has led me to imagine might not have been unacceptable to Him who heareth prayer. At all events, I date my conversion, and my awakening to a new life—a consciousness of superior powers and a destiny to anything I had before conceived of—from this day, so memorable to me. I used every means and opportunity of inquiry into religious matters; and so deep was my conviction of their superior importance to everything else, so clear my perception of my own faults, and so undoubting my observation of the darkness and sin that surrounded me, that I could not help talking much on these subjects with those about me; and it was not long before I began to pray with them, and exhort them, and to impart to the poor slaves those little glimmerings of light from another world, which had reached my own eye.

"My master's habits were such as were common enough among the dissipated planters of the neighbourhood; and one of their frequent practices was, to assemble on Saturday or Sunday, which were their holidays, and gamble, run horses, or fight game-cocks, discuss politics, and drink whisky, and brandy and water, all day long. Perfectly aware that they would not be able to find their own way home at night, each one ordered a slave, his particular attendant, to come after him and help him home. I was chosen for this confidential duty by my master; and many is the time I have held him on his horse, when he could not hold himself in the saddle, and walked by his side in darkness and mud from the tavern to his house. Of course, quarrels and brawls of the most violent description were frequent consequences of these meetings, and whenever they became especially dangerous, and glasses were thrown, dirks drawn, and pistols fired, it was the duty of the slaves to rush in, and each one was to drag his master from the fight, and carry him home.

"On one of these occasions, my master got into a quarrel with his brother's overseer, whose name was Bryce Litton, who was one of the party, and in rescuing the former, I suppose I was a little more rough with the latter than usual. I remember his falling upon the floor, and very likely it was from the effects of a push from me, or a movement of my elbow. He attributed his fall to me, rather than to the whisky he had drunk, and treasured up his vengeance for the first favourable opportunity. About a week afterwards, I was sent by my master to a place a few miles distant, on horseback, with some letters. I took a short cut through a lane, separated by gates from the high road, and bounded by a fence on each side. This lane passed through some of the farm owned by my master's brother, and his overseer was in the adjoining field, with three negroes, when I went by. On my return, half an hour afterwards, the overseer was sitting on the fence; but I could see nothing of the black fellows. I rode on, utterly unsuspicious of any trouble, but as I approached, he jumped off the fence, and at the same moment two of the negroes sprang up from under the bushes, where they had been concealed, and stood with him, immediately in front of me; while the third sprang over the fence just behind me. The overseer seized my horse's bridle, and ordered me to alight. I asked what I was to alight for. 'To take the cursedest flogging you ever had in your life, you d———d black scoundrel.' 'But what am I to be flogged for, Mr Litton?' I asked. 'Not a word,' said he, 'but 'light at once, and take off your jacket.' I saw there was nothing else to be done, and slipped off the horse on the opposite side from him. 'Now take off your shirt,' cried he; and as I demurred at this, he lifted a stick he had in his hand to strike me, but so suddenly and violently, that he frightened the horse, which broke away from him, and ran home. I was thus left without means of escape, to sustain the attacks of four men, as well as I might. In avoiding Mr Litton's blow, I had accidentally got into a corner of the fence, where I could not be approached except in front. The overseer called upon the negroes to seize me; but they, knowing something of my physical power, were rather slow to obey. At length they did their best, and as they brought themselves within my reach, I knocked them down successively; and one of them trying to trip up my feet when he was down,

I gave him a kick with my heavy shoe, which knocked out several of his front teeth, and sent him groaning away. Meanwhile, the cowardly overseer was availing himself of every opportunity to hit me over the head with his stick, which was not heavy enough to knock me down, though it drew blood freely. At length, tired of the length of the affray, he seized a stake, six or seven feet long, from the fence, and struck at me with his whole strength. In attempting to ward off the blow, my right arm was broken, and I was brought to the ground; where repeated blows broke both my shoulder-blades, and made the blood gush from my mouth copiously. The two blacks begged him not to murder me, and he just left me as I was, telling me to learn what it was to strike a white man. The alarm had been raised at the house, by seeing the horse come back without his rider, and it was not long before assistance arrived to convey me home. It may be supposed it was not done without some suffering on my part; as, besides my broken arm and the wounds on my head, I could feel and hear the pieces of my shoulder-blades grate against each other with every breath. No physician or surgeon was called to dress my wounds, and I never knew one to be called to a slave upon Riley's estate, on any occasion whatever, and have no knowledge of such a thing being done on any estate in the neighbourhood. I was attended, if it may be called attendance, by my master's sister, who had some reputation in such affairs; and she splintered my arm, and bound up my back as well as she knew how, and nature did the rest. It was five months before I could work at all, and the first time I tried to plough, a hard knock of the coulter against a stone shattered my shoulder-blades again, and gave me even greater agony than at first. I have been unable to raise my hands to my head from that day to this. My master prosecuted Mr Litton for abusing and maiming his slave; and when the case was tried before the magistrate, he made a statement of the facts as I have here related them. When Mr Litton was called upon to say why he should not be fined for the offence, he simply stated, without being put on oath, that he had acted in self-defence; that I had assaulted him; and that nothing had saved him from being killed on the spot by so stout a fellow, but the fortunate circumstance that his three negroes were within call. The result was, that my master paid all the costs of court.

"My situation as overseer I retained, together with the especial favour of my master, who was not displeased either with saving the expense of a large salary for a white superintendent, or with the superior crops I was able to raise for him.

"When I was about twenty-two years of age, I married a very efficient, and, for a slave, a very well-taught girl, belonging to a neighbouring family, reputed to be pious and kind, whom I first met at the chapel I attended; and during nearly forty years that have since elapsed, I have had no reason to regret the connexion, but many to rejoice in it, and be grateful for it.

"Things remained in this condition for a considerable

period; my occupations being to superintend the farming operations, and to sell the produce in the neighbouring markets of Washington and Georgetown.

"After a time, however, continual dissipation was more than a match for domestic saving. My master fell into difficulty. He then told me I must take his slaves to his brother, in Kentucky. There were eighteen negroes, besides my wife, two children, and myself, to transport a thousand miles, through a country I knew nothing about, and in winter time, for we started in the month of February 1825. My master proposed to follow me in a few months, and establish himself in Kentucky. He furnished me with a small sum of money, and some provisions; and I bought a one-horse waggon, to carry them, and to give the women and children a lift now and then, and the rest of us were to trudge on foot.

"On arriving at Wheeling, I sold the horse and waggon, and purchased a boat of sufficient size, and floated down the river without further trouble or fatigue, stopping every night to encamp.

"In passing along the State of Ohio, we were frequently told that we were free, if we chose to be so. At Cincinnati, especially, the coloured people gathered round us, and urged us with much importunity to remain with them. From my earliest recollection, freedom had been the object of my ambition, a constant motive to exertion, an ever-present stimulus to gain and to save. No other means of obtaining it, however, had occurred to me but purchasing myself of my master.

The idea of running away was not one that I had ever indulged. I had a sentiment of honour on the subject, or what I thought such, which I would not have violated even for freedom; and every cent which I had ever felt entitled to call my own had been treasured up for this great purpose, till I had accumulated between thirty and forty dollars. Now was offered to me an opportunity I had not anticipated. I might liberate my family, my companions, and myself, without the smallest risk, and without injustice to any individual, except one whom we had none of us any reason to love, who had been guilty of cruelty and oppression to us all for many years, and who had never shewn the smallest symptom of sympathy with us, or with any one in our condition.

"But I had promised that man to take his property to Kentucky, and deposit it with his brother; and this only I resolved to do. I have often had painful doubts as to the propriety of my carrying so many other individuals into slavery again, and my consoling reflection has been, that I acted as I thought at the time was best.

"I arrived at Davies county, Kentucky, about the middle of April 1825, and delivered myself and my companions to Mr Amos Riley, the brother of my owner, who had a large plantation, with from eighty to one hundred negroes. His house was situated about five miles south of the Ohio River, and fifteen miles above the Yellow Banks, on Big Blackford's Creek. There I remained three years, expecting my master to follow; and employed meantime on the farm, of which I had the general management, in consequence of the recommendation for ability and honesty which I brought with me from Maryland. My post of superintendent gave me some advantages, too, of which, I did not fail to avail myself, particularly with regard to those religious privileges, which, since I first heard of Christ and Christianity, had greatly occupied my mind. In Kentucky, the opportunities of attending on the preaching of whites, as well as of blacks, were more numerous.

"In the course of the three years from 1825 to 1828, I availed myself of all the opportunities of improvement which occurred, and was admitted as a preacher by a Conference of the Methodist Episcopal Church.

"In the spring of the year 1828, news arrived from my master that he was unable to induce his wife to accompany him to Kentucky, and he must therefore remain where he was. He sent out an agent to sell all his slaves but me and my family, and to carry back the proceeds to him. And now another of those heart-rending scenes was to be witnessed, which had impressed itself so deeply on my childish soul. Husbands and wives, parents and children, were to be separated for ever. Affections, which are as strong in the African as in the European, were to be cruelly disregarded; and the iron selfishness generated by the hateful 'institution' was to be exhibited in its most odious and naked deformity. I was exempted from a personal share in the dreadful calamity, but I could not see, without the deepest grief, the agony which I recollected in my own mother, and which was again brought before my eyes in the persons with whom I had been long associated; nor could I refrain from the bitterest feeling of hatred of the system and those who sustain it.

"In the course of the summer of 1828, a Methodist preacher said, 'If you will obtain Mr Amos's consent to go to see your old master in Maryland, I will try and put you in a way by which I think you may succeed in buying yourself.' Somewhat to my surprise, Mr Amos gave me a pass to go to Maryland and back. Furnished with this, and with a letter of recommendation from my Methodist friend to a brother preacher in Cincinnati, I started about the middle of September 1828 for the east. By the aid of the good man to whom I had a letter, I had an opportunity of preaching in two or three of the pulpits of Cincinnati, when I took the opportunity of stating my purpose, and was liberally aided in it by contributions made on the spot. I succeeded so well, that when I arrived at Montgomery county, I was master of two hundred and seventy-five dollars, besides my horse and my clothes. My master was surprised to see me dressed and mounted in so respectable style. Amid expressions of an apparently cordial welcome, I could discern, plainly enough, the look of displeasure that a slave should have got possession of such luxuries.

"I found my mother had died during my absence, and every tie which had ever connected me with this place was broken.

"My master agreed to give me my manumission papers for four hundred and fifty dollars, of which three hundred and fifty dollars were to be in cash, and the remainder in my note. My money and my horse enabled me to pay the cash at once, and thus my great hopes seemed in a fair way of being realised.

"Some time was spent in the negotiations for this affair, and it was not till the 9th of March 1829 that I received my manumission papers in due form of law. I was prepared to start immediately on my return to Kentucky, and on the 10th, as I was getting ready in the morning for my journey, my master accosted me in a very pleasant and friendly manner, and entered into conversation with me about my plans. He asked me what I was going to do with my freedom certificate; whether I was going to shew it, if I were questioned on the road. I told him yes, that I supposed it was given to me for that very purpose. 'Ah,' said he, 'you do not understand the dangers to which you are exposed. You may meet with some ruffianly slave-purchaser who will rob you of that piece of paper, and destroy it. You will then be thrown into prison, and sold for your gaol fees, before any of your friends can know it. Why should you shew it at all? You can go to Kentucky in perfect safety with your pass. Let me enclose that valuable document for you under cover to my brother, and nobody will dare to break a seal, for that is a State-prison matter; and when you arrive in Kentucky you will have it all safe and sound.' This seemed most friendly advice, and I felt very grateful for his kindness. I accordingly saw him enclose my precious piece of paper in two or three envelopes, seal it with three seals, and direct it to his brother in Davies county, Kentucky, in my care. Leaving immediately for Wheeling, to which place I was obliged to travel on foot, I there took boat, and in due time reached my destination.

"I went directly to my own cabin, where I found my wife and little ones well; and, of course, we had a good deal to communicate to each other. Letters had reached the 'great house,' as the master's was always called, long before I had arrived, telling them what I had been doing; and the children of the family had been eager to communicate the great news to my wife,— how I had been preaching, and raising money, and making a bargain for my freedom. It was not long before Charlotte began to tell me with much excitement what she had heard, and to question me about how I had raised the money I had paid, and how I expected to get the remainder of the *thousand dollars* I was to give for my freedom. I could scarcely believe my ears; but, before telling her how the case exactly was, I questioned her again and again as to what she had heard. She persisted in repeating the same story as she had heard it from my master's letters, and I began to perceive the trick that had been played upon me, and to see the management by which Isaac Riley had contrived that the only evidence of my freedom should be kept from every eye but that of his brother Amos, who was instructed to retain it till I had made up six hundred and fifty dollars, the balance I was reported to have agreed to pay.

"The next morning I went up to the house, and shewed myself to Mr Amos, who was really glad to see me, as my time and labour were important to him. We had a long conversation, and, after rallying me, as his brother had done, about my being turned fine gentleman, he told me what Isaac had written to him about the price I was to pay, how much I had already made up, &c. I found my wife was right. 'But,' said he, 'you have given too much for yourself. Isaac has been too hard upon you, and I don't see how you are going to get so much in Kentucky.'

"Things went on as usual for about a year, when, one day, Mr Amos told me that I must get ready to go to New Orleans with his son Amos, a young man about twenty-one years of age, who was going down the river with a flat boat, and was nearly ready to start; in fact, he was to leave the next day, and I must go and take care of him, and help him to dispose of the cargo. The intimation was enough. Though it was not distinctly stated, yet I well knew what was intended, and my heart sunk within me at the near prospect of this fatal blight to all my long-cherished hopes.

"In a few days we arrived in New Orleans, and the little that remained of our cargo was soon sold, the men were discharged, and nothing was left but to dispose of me, and break up the boat, and then Mr Amos would take passage on a steamboat, and go home. There was no longer any disguise about the purpose of selling me. Mr Amos acknowledged that such were his instructions, and he set about fulfilling them. Several planters came to the boat to look at me; and I was sent off some hasty errand, that they might see how I could run. My points were canvassed as those of a horse would have been. The boat was to be sold, and I was to be sold, the next day, and Amos was to set off on his return, at six o'clock in the afternoon.

"A little before daylight Mr Amos awoke indisposed. His stomach was disordered; but he lay down again, thinking it would pass off. In a little while he was up again, and felt more sick than before, and it was soon evident that the river fever was upon him. He became rapidly worse, and by eight o'clock in the morning he was utterly prostrate; his head was on my lap, and he was begging me to help him, to do something for him, to save him. He entreated me to despatch matters, to sell the flat boat, in which we two had been living by ourselves for some days, and to get him and his trunk, containing the proceeds of the trip, on board the steamer as quick as possible, and especially not to desert him so long as he lived, nor to suffer his body, if he died, to be thrown into the river. I attended to all his requests, and by twelve o'clock that day he was in one of the cabins of the steamer appropriated to sick passengers.

"All was done which could be done for the comfort and relief of any one in such a desperate condition.

But he was reduced to extremity. He ceased to grow worse after a day or two, and he must speedily have died if he had not; but his strength was so entirely gone, that he could neither speak nor move a limb, and could only indicate his wish for a teaspoonful of gruel, or something to moisten his throat, by a feeble motion of his lips. I nursed him carefully and constantly. Nothing else could have saved his life. It hung by a thread for a long time. We were as much as twelve days in reaching home.

"We arrived home about the 10th of July, but it was not till the middle of August that Amos was well enough to move out of his chamber, though he had been convalescent all the while. As soon as he could speak, he told all I had done for him, and said, 'If I had sold him, I should have died;' but it never seemed to occur to him or the rest of the family that they were under any, the slightest, obligation to me on that account. As soon as Amos began to recover, I began to meditate upon a plan of escape from the danger, in which I constantly stood, of a repetition of the attempt to sell me in the highest market. Providence seemed to have interfered once to defeat the scheme; but I could not expect such extraordinary circumstances to be repeated, and I was bound to do everything in my power to secure myself and my family from the wicked conspiracy of Isaac and Amos Riley against my life, as well as against my natural rights in my own person, and those which I had acquired, under even the barbarous laws of slavery, by the money I had paid for myself. If Isaac would only have been honest enough to adhere to his own bargain, I would have adhered to mine, and paid him all I had promised. But his attempt to kidnap me again, after having pocketed three-fourths of my market value, absolved me from all obligation, in my opinion, to pay him any more, or to continue in a position which exposed me to his machinations. I determined to make my escape to Canada, about which I had heard something, as beyond the limits of the United States; for, notwithstanding there were Free States in the Union, I felt that I should be safer under an entirely foreign jurisdiction. The Slave States had their emissaries in the others, and I feared that I might fall into their hands, and need a stronger protection than might be afforded me by public opinion in the Northern States at that time.

"It was not without long thought on the subject that I devised a plan of escape; but when I had fully made up my mind, I communicated my intention to my wife, who was too much terrified by the dangers of the attempt to do anything, at first, but endeavour to dissuade me from it, and try to make me contented with my condition as it was. In vain I explained to her the liability we were in of being separated from our children as well as from each other; and presented every argument which had weighed with my own mind, and had at last decided me. She had not gone through my trials, and female timidity overcame her sense of the evils she had experienced. I argued the matter with her, at various times, till I was satisfied that argument alone would not prevail; and then I said to her, very deliberately, that though it was a cruel thing for me to part with her, yet I would do it, and take all the children with me but the youngest, rather than run the risk of a forcible separation from them all, and of a much worse captivity besides, which we were constantly exposed to here. She wept and entreated, but found I was resolute, and after a whole night spent in talking over the matter, I left her to go to my work for the day. I had not gone far when I heard her voice calling me;—I waited till she came up to me, and then, finding me as determined as ever, she said, at last, she would go with me. It was an immense relief to me, and my tears flowed as fast as hers had done before. I rode off with a heart a good deal lighter.

"She was living, at the time, near the landing I have mentioned; for the plantation extended the whole five miles from the house to the river, and there were several different farms, all of which I was overseeing, and, therefore, riding about from one to another every day. The oldest boy was at the house with Mr Amos, the rest were all with her. Her consent was given on Thursday morning, and on the night of the following Saturday, I had decided to set out, as it would then be several days before I should be missed, and I should get a good start. Some time previously I had got my wife to make me a large knapsack, big enough to hold the two smallest children; and I had arranged it that she should lead the second boy, while the oldest was stout enough to go by himself, and to help me to carry the necessary food. I used to pack the little ones on my back, of an evening, after I had got through my day's work, and trot round the cabin with them, and go some little distance from it, in order to accustom both them and myself to the task before us.

"At length the eventful night came. I went up to the house to ask leave to take Tom home with me, that he might have his clothes mended. No objection was made, and I bade Master Amos 'good night' for the last time. It was about the middle of September, and by nine o'clock in the evening all was ready. It was a dark, moonless night, and we got into the little skiff in which I had induced a fellow-slave to take us across the Ohio River. It was an agitating and solemn moment. The good fellow who was rowing us over said this affair might end in his death. 'But,' said he, 'you will not be brought back alive, will you?' 'Not if I can help it,' I answered. 'And if you are overpowered and return,' he asked, 'will you conceal my part of the business?' 'That I will, so help me God,' I replied. 'Then I am easy,' he answered, 'and wish you success.' We landed on the Indiana shore, and I began to feel that I was my own master. But in what circumstances of fear and misery still! We were to travel by night, and rest by day in the woods and bushes. We were thrown absolutely upon our own poor and small resources, and were to rely on our own strength alone. The population was not so numerous as now, nor so well disposed to the slave. We dared look to no one for help. But my courage was equal to the occasion, and we trudged on cautiously and steadily, and as fast as the darkness and the feebleness of my wife and boys would allow.

"When I got on the Canada side, on the morning of the 28th of October 1830, my first impulse was to throw myself on the ground, and, giving way to the riotous exultation of my feelings, to execute sundry antics which excited the astonishment of those who were looking on. A gentleman of the neighbourhood, Colonel Warren, who happened to be present, thought I was in a fit, and as he inquired what was the matter with the poor fellow, I jumped up and told him, *I was free!* 'Oh!' said he, with a hearty laugh, 'is that it? I never knew freedom make a man roll in the sand before.' It is not much to be wondered at, that my certainty of being free was not quite a sober one at the first moment: and I hugged and kissed my wife and children all round, with a vivacity which made them laugh as well as myself."

SECTION XI.—THE WILL OF GOD RESPECTING SLAVERY.

The slavery which was allowed by God to the Israelites affords no sanction to American slavery, for the following reasons:—

God having, for wise and good reasons, permitted it to them, it became *on that account* lawful; whereas it is unlawful under Christian governments, because He has given them no such permission. Actions may be right when appointed by Him, which would be wrong without such appointment. Abraham did right when, in obedience to the command of God, he prepared to take the life of his son; whereas if he had taken it without such command he would have been a murderer. God, who has the right over human life, saw fit to punish the Canaanites for their sins by ordering the Israelites to exterminate those of them whom they conquered, (Deut. vii. 2, 3.) The soldiers of Israel were bound to obey His commands. But the slaughter which, under His orders, was simply an act of duty, would have been without such order cruelty. Exactly the same may be said of this slave system. For the best reasons, God allowed them to buy slaves of their heathen neighbours, (Lev. xxv. 44–46,) which but for that express permission they could not have done without injustice.

Had the Africans been like the Canaanites, preeminently sinners, and had the American slave-holders received from God an express permission to enslave them, they might have been guiltless; but in the absence of a Divine enactment addressed to them, they have no more right to enslave the Africans than they have to exterminate them.

As the Israelites, by the law of God, held certain persons in bondage, so by the same law they killed the Canaanites whom they took in battle, and stoned to death a man who picked up sticks on the Sabbath-day. If their example gives authority to the slave-holder in the one case, it does also in the other two. If the

Virginian legislature plead Divine authority for enslaving their fellow-men, they may equally plead it for killing every man whom they take in battle, or for executing every one of their own citizens who picks up sticks on the Sabbath. The judicial code of the Hebrews, suited to other times and circumstances, has passed away, and can no more sanction in Virginia the slavery of the Africans than it does the murder of idolaters or of Sabbath-breakers.

On other grounds, the slavery practised by the Israelites fails to justify that which prevails in America. According to the law of Moses, idolaters might be bought who were previously slaves; but no freeman might be seized and sold under pain of death, (Lev. xxv. 44; Exod. xxi. 16.) Freemen, therefore, and their children could not be reduced to a state of bondage. Freemen or their children held in slavery, if any such there were, were held contrary to law. And, therefore, the slavery of the negroes, who are nearly all children of freemen originally kidnapped, ought by the Mosaic law to be declared free.

Further, the slavery allowed by God in Israel cannot be pleaded by American slave-holders as a precedent, because the reasons on which it was founded no longer exist. The Israelites being prone to idolatry, God saw fit to guard them against this sin by very severe enactments against idolaters. The idolatrous Canaanites, and then all the Israelites who fell into idolatry, were to be put to death,* that His worshippers

* Deut. vii. 2, 3, xiii. 6, 10, 12, 16, xvii. 2.

might see how He abhors idolatry. And when He permitted some of them to be made slaves, it was for the same purpose. But that object has ceased. Gentlemen in Virginia are not in danger of adopting African superstitions, as the Israelites were of worshipping Baal or Astarte; and the reason for the enslavement of the Canaanites not applying to the Africans, they cannot plead that the permission to hold slaves given to the Israelites extends to them. But in the absence of such permission, we have no more right to enslave Africans because the Israelites under orders enslaved the Canaanites, than we have a right to kill Africans because the Israelites under orders killed the Canaanites. Finally, God ordered that all slaves should be liberated at the jubilee: "*Ye shall hallow the fiftieth year, and proclaim liberty throughout all the land* UNTO ALL THE INHABITANTS THEREOF," (Lev. xxv. 10.) If the Mosaic law is adopted as a precedent, it should be taken entire; and then each slave in the Slave States ought to be set free, because the fiftieth year of American slavery has long since passed.

But, further, the Hebrew slave system expressly condemns the American slave-holders; for this was then the law of God: "*If thy brother that dwelleth by thee be waxen poor, and be sold unto thee; thou shalt not compel him to serve as a bond-servant. . . . .* FOR THEY ARE MY SERVANTS, *which I brought forth out of the land of Egypt: they shall not be sold as bondmen,*" (Lev. xxv. 39, 42.) God would not allow any Israelites to be made slaves, *because they were His servants*. But the relations of Christians to each other being much closer than that of an Israelite to his fellow-citizen, and a Christian being as much nearer to God than an Israelite, as a son is nearer to a father than a servant is, (Gal. iv. 3-7,) His order that no Israelite should be a slave must *à fortiori* apply to every Christian.

No less difficult is it for the slave-holders to extract a justification of their system from the silence of the New Testament respecting Roman slavery.

If the legislatures of the Slave States may maintain a slave system because the Roman emperors did so, they may no less establish an autocratic despotism, engage in lawless wars, impose arbitrary taxes, and rule by military violence, because the emperors did all these things. The silence of Jesus and His apostles respecting these crimes, must establish their lawfulness as much as His silence respecting their slave system can establish its lawfulness. A Christian government must not commit the crimes which a brutal and bloody heathen government committed, because the New Testament did not speak of them.

Nor may Christians, under a Christian government, hold slaves, because Christians under a heathen government did so without rebuke. Onesimus was sent back to his master from motives of compassion to Christian slaves. Had these been declared by Paul free, and encouraged to run away from their masters, their condition throughout the empire would have become much worse than it was. Each heathen master would have seen in them those who denied his authority, and would have taken new precautions to prevent their escape. The silence of the apostle was forced upon him by the fear that he would, by interference, make their condition worse. And if Christian masters were not ordered to manumit their slaves, it was for a similar reason. For the duty of the master would have carried with it the right of the slave; and if the apostles had thus proclaimed that every slave had a right to his freedom, we may infer, from the wrath lately evinced at Richmond, with what hatred the slave-holders would have denounced the Christian doctrine, and with what fury they would have persecuted the Christian slave.

Jewish and Romish slave-holders were in circumstances little resembling those of the slave-holders in the American Confederation. A class much more nearly resembling them were the Egyptian slave-holders, who enslaved the Israelites simply because they had the power to do so. Like the negroes of Virginia and of South Carolina, the Israelites having suffered many wrongs, "*they sighed by reason of their bondage; and they cried, and their cry came up unto God by reason of their bondage.*" "*And the Lord said, I have surely seen the affliction of my people which are in Egypt, and have heard their cry by reason of their taskmasters; for I know their sorrows; and I am come down to deliver them out of the hand of the Egyptians.*"*

In our day the negroes, among whom are many children of God, have taken the place of the oppressed

* Exod. ii. 23, iii. 7, 8.

Israelites; the slave-holders of the Confederation are in the condition of the Egyptian oppressors; and now a second time has the cry of the oppressed against the oppressors reached the ear of God.

In appealing to the New Testament, the slave-holders have secured their own condemnation. Their whole system is a gigantic robbery, by which they have taken from four millions of working men and women their most precious rights; and the apostle Paul has said, "*Know ye not that the unrighteous shall not inherit the kingdom of God? Be not deceived: neither fornicators, nor adulterers, nor thieves, shall inherit the kingdom of God,*" (1 Cor. vi. 9, 10.)

Although Jesus, by His apostle Paul, said to masters, even under the Roman system, "*Masters, give unto your servants that which is just and equal,*" (Col. iv. 1,) they have extorted from them daily eleven hours of labour, without giving them wages for their work.

For the millions of bales which they have heaped into their barns, and the hundreds of millions sterling with which they have filled their pockets, they have given to the producers of all this wealth the coarsest food, the cheapest clothing, and the poorest huts; and Jesus, by His servant James, has said to them, "*Behold, the hire of the labourers who have reaped down your fields, which is of you kept back by fraud, crieth: and the cries of them which have reaped are entered into the ears of the Lord of sabaoth. Ye have lived in pleasure on the earth, and been wanton; ye have nourished your hearts, as in a day of slaughter,"* (James v. 4, 5.)

The cruelties, so diversified and so innumerable, which have been inflicted upon these unresisting sufferers, have not been unnoticed. Whips soaked in their blood—their mangled flesh—their writhing bodies—their limbs loaded with handcuffs — men tortured in secret and driven by their misery to suicide—men dying by inches in chains, or torn by dogs, or mutilated by diabolic rage, or burned alive before exulting crowds—all have been seen by Him who has, by His apostle, said of their murderers: "*The works of the flesh are manifest, which are these: Adultery, fornication, hatred, wrath, murders: of the which I tell you before, that they which do such things shall not inherit the kingdom of God,*" (Gal. v. 19–22.)

Lawless men, who have made women their chattels, and by their resistless power have corrupted them, till nearly one-fourth of the coloured race in the Slave States bears the mark of their profligacy, have not escaped their Judge. Slave-holders who prohibit marriage, which God has commanded, and practise fornication, which He has forbidden, have their accounts to settle with Him. Preachers of the South may flatter the adulterous oligarch, and the churches of the South may fawn upon him; but Jesus, by His apostle, has said: "*The unbelieving, and the abominable, and murderers, and whoremongers, shall have their part in the lake which burneth with fire and brimstone,*" (Rev. xxi. 8.)

Further, the condemnation which Jesus has pronounced upon those sins, which are the hideous creations of a system of absolute power, on the one hand, and of defenceless subjection, on the other, extends to the whole system. His principles are opposed to the principles of the slave-holders; His justice to their oppression; and His law of kindness to their systematic cruelty.

What is the grand law which Jesus has enacted to govern every Slave State, to direct every legislature, and to order the family of every slave-holder? "*As ye would that men should do to you, do ye also to them likewise,*" (Luke vi. 31.) Slave-holders, what would you wish a superior to do to you? You would wish him to leave to you the free use of your mind and limbs, to allow you fair wages for your work, to let you seek your own happiness in your own way, and to get all the knowledge which might make you a better and a happier man. All this that you would ask from a superior you are bound by the law of Christ to do for your labourers; and as long as you refuse to do it for them, you are deliberately and systematically despising His authority.

Further, He has promulgated a law of kindness which, no less than the law of justice, ought to govern every slave-holder in his home, on his estate, and in all his public acts. Two great commands determine what ought to be our prevailing tempers: "*Thou shalt love the Lord thy God with all thy heart; and thou shalt love thy neighbour as thyself,*" (Matt. xxii. 37, 39.)

The second of these two commands was thus expounded by Jesus to a lawyer who asked him its meaning: "A certain man went down from Jerusalem to Jericho, and fell among thieves, who stripped him of his raiment, and wounded him, and departed, leaving him half dead. A certain Samaritan, as he journeyed, came where he was: and when he saw him, he had compassion on him, and went to him, and bound up his wounds, pouring in oil and wine, and set him on his own beast, and brought him to an inn, and took care of him. And on the morrow when he departed, he took out two pence, and gave them to the host, and said unto him, Take care of him; and whatever thou spendest more, when I come again, I will repay thee. Go, and do thou likewise," (Luke x. 30, 33–37.) Slave-holder, you have found four millions of slaves stripped of their comforts, and helpless in their misery. Jesus bids you be the good Samaritan to some of them. For this is to love your neighbour as yourself. For if you love your labourer with a benevolence as true, as irrespective of faults, as patient and as persevering as the regard which you bear to yourself, you will try to raise him from misery to freedom, knowledge, and happiness, as you would try to raise yourself.

Yet even so you have not done all which your Master in heaven requires of you; for if you profess to be a Christian, you must regard many of these negroes as your fellow-disciples. Observe, then, the law which regulates your duty to them: "*A new commandment I give unto you, That ye love one* another; as I have loved you, that ye also love one another. By this shall all men know that ye are my disciples, if ye have love one to another," (John xiii. 34;) "All ye are brothers," (Matt. xxiii. 9;) "There is neither Jew nor Greek, there is neither bond nor free: for ye are all one in Christ Jesus," (Gal. iii. 28.)

"Love as brothers," (1 Pet. iii. 6.) You are a brother to your Christian negroes, and they are brothers to you; can you extort labour from them without wages? Can you drive them with the whip, feed them on the coarsest fare, dress them in the poorest clothing, lodge them in the meanest huts, shut them out from all knowledge, and shoot them on the slightest resistance? That would not be loving them as brothers. If you do not wish to be publicly rejected, as having no love to Him, because you have no love to them, you will change your whole conduct to them. One day He will come again in His glory. On His right hand will stand those Christian slaves, while you, unless you repent, will be on the left. On that occasion there will be no distinction between master and slave; and He has told you beforehand what judgment you must expect if you have neglected to shew kindness to those slaves whom He will then own as His brothers: "*Then shall he say to them on the left hand, Depart from me, ye cursed, into everlasting fire, prepared for the devil and his angels: for I was an hungered, and ye gave me no meat: I was thirsty, and ye gave me no drink: I was a stranger, and ye took me not in: naked, and ye clothed me not: sick, and in prison, and ye visited me not. Verily I say unto you, Inasmuch as ye did it not to one of the least of these, ye did it not to me,"* (Matt. xxv. 41.) If that will be the effect of mere indifference to them when misused by others, what will be your doom if you have yourself robbed, flogged, pauperised, and degraded them, kept them in rags and dirt, debarred them from all earthly happiness, filled their lives with hardships, and been the chief author of their sorrows and their sins?

From the law of Jesus let us turn to His life, for we are no less bound to imitate His example than we are to obey His commands. His own words are, "*I have given you an example that ye should do as I have done to you." " As I have loved you, that ye also love one another."** "*He that saith he abideth in him, ought himself also so to walk even as he walked."*†

Jesus our Saviour has set us the example of a love which passes knowledge.‡ From the highest glory He descended to the cross to rescue us from the chains of sin, and from the tyranny of the devil.§ To accomplish this work He became so poor that He had not an acre of land, nor a house of His own, nor money to pay tribute to the temple, nor food for His hunger; but was fed by the alms of a few disciples: and when He died, was laid in another man's grave. "*Ye know the grace of our Lord Jesus Christ, that though he was rich, yet for your sakes he became poor, that ye*

---

* John xiii. 15, 34. † 1 John ii. 6.
‡ Eph. iii. 19. § Phil. ii. 5.

through his poverty might be rich." All this poverty He suffered to enrich us with pardon, wisdom, righteousness, holiness, the gift of His Spirit, peace on earth, and an eternal home in heaven. If He lodged in poor cottages, travelled many hundreds of miles on foot, and endured various hardships, it was that He might say to all sin-burdened men, *"Come unto me, all ye that labour and are heavy laden, and I will give you rest."*† Although He inflicted no pain, He suffered much for our sakes; and when He died, by His own consent, amidst universal scorn and hatred, upon the cross, He was voluntarily paying the awful price which was to set us free from guilt and wrath. *"Christ hath redeemed us from the curse of the law, being made a curse for us."*‡ In working out our salvation, He was "holy, harmless, undefiled, and separate from sinners." Not a single defect detracted from the loveliness of His character; and by the death which followed that blameless life, *"he gave himself for us, that he might redeem us from all iniquity, and purify unto himself a peculiar people, zealous of good works."*§

But, not content with saving us from hell and from sin, He feels a benevolent satisfaction in raising all His disciples to share with Him in the joy of heaven. *"Christ loved the church, and gave himself for it, that he might present it to himself a glorious church."* ‖ Ought we not, then, as Christians, to make our fellow-Christians as happy as we can?

* 2 Cor. viii. 9.   † Matt. xi. 28.   ‡ Gal. iii. 10, 13.
§ Titus ii. 14.   ‖ Eph. v. 25, 27.

Though slave-holders bear His name, do they act like Him? He humbled Himself that He might make millions of slaves freemen; and they exalt themselves by making millions of freemen slaves. He who created the worlds, and now rules over them, made himself poor that He might enrich the needy; they have made themselves rich by stealing from the needy all that they possessed. He bore stripes and shame to make the miserable happy; they inflict stripes and shame to make the happy miserable. He sacrificed His own life to save the wicked; they sacrifice the lives of the innocent to gratify themselves. He came down from heaven to earth that He might raise the weak from hell to heaven; they have raised themselves to dignity and dominion by reducing the weak to physical, mental, and moral degradation. Yet when, by their slave system, they have despised His authority, trampled on His laws, rejected His example, and dishonoured His name, they claim Him as the patron of their abomination. Not content with making millions miserable through their greed, and thereby degrading their poorer neighbours, and ruining the morals of their children, they must drag Christianity through the dirt, support by the pretended authority of Jesus a crime which He abhors, tempt inconsiderate men to infidelity by linking Christian doctrine to lawless oppression, and bring the name of Jesus, which is above every name in earth or heaven, the name of our Redeemer, Mediator, and Saviour, to be sneered at and abhorred.

May England never aid these men in their wickedness!

RECAPITULATION.

WITH the freemen of the Northern States we have every reason to sympathise. The people are happy, the laws are just, the government is beneficent; there is much godliness in the land, and their efforts to promote the knowledge and fear of God throughout all the population have excited the admiration of all who have known them. Wild hordes, steeped in superstition, or fired with revolutionary frenzy, whom Europe has discharged upon their coast, have been enlightened and transformed. Their missionaries have helped ours to preach Christ in India and China, in Syria, in the Turkish empire; and only four years ago God blessed them by a great work of His Spirit, in all the Free States, in which tens of thousands became His servants through faith in Jesus. I should think it a disgrace not to be interested in the welfare of a people among whom there is so much freedom, intelligence, order, and godliness, of whom so many love the Saviour, and whom God has so pre-eminently blessed.

Let us now turn to the Slave States who are in rebellion. Of that rebellion I shall speak in another work. Without, therefore, introducing any comments upon it here, I will recapitulate the chief features of that slaveholding society which now asks for sympathy and recognition.

Excluding those of the Border States who remain faithful to the Union, and who, breathing its purer atmosphere, will soon, I trust, hate slavery as it does, the eleven Confederate States have a population of 5,581,649 whites, and 3,520,116 slaves, being in all 9,101,765. Of these we may say in round numbers that there are two hundred thousand slave-holders, who with their families may amount to one million; one hundred and fifty thousand slave-hirers, who with their families may reach the number of seven hundred and fifty thousand; about four millions of mean whites, and about three millions and a-half of slaves. With republican forms of government, the two hundred thousand slave-holders form an oligarchy which has ruled the other three classes. They alone have an interest in slavery; but, being aided by the slave-hirers, who have many affinities with them, they lead the "mean whites" as they will.

The slave system is most elaborately contrived to place the working-classes under their feet. They can sell their labourers, part them from their families, tearing asunder all their dearest ties, work them without relaxation, feed them or starve them at their pleasure, clothe them or make them shiver in rags, insult them by brutal language, strike them without dread of resistance, flog them without mercy, and kill them on the smallest provocation. Whatever outrages they may commit against the wives and daughters of their labourers, the law gives them impunity by declaring that these wives and daughters belong to them as much as their cows or their pigs do.

They are safe whatever violent crimes they may commit, because no magistrate may receive the testimony of their working-men against them. Fifty labourers may see a woman flogged to death by her master without daring to whisper a word about it, because their imprudence would expose them to be similarly treated by the incensed murderer. Insults, wrongs, and cruelties may be perpetrated every hour on an estate by the owner without the world knowing any more of them than it does of the groans and the torments of the damned. Hundreds and thousands may say of these plantations what an old man said to Linda Brent,—"It is hell in missis' house; day and night I prays to die;" yet no one can hear them. Europe cannot know, nor Massachusetts, nor even humane Southerners. Ruffians on their plantations may spend their lives in tormenting the innocent; and despair may dwell in innumerable cabins, while an impenetrable secrecy shrouds the whole region.

To complete their power, by rendering those whom they work as beasts more bestial than the cart-whip alone could make them, the slave-holders have forbidden their working-men to read. It was not impiety enough to found their empire upon the contempt of marriage, declaring that no labourer should have a legal wife; and, therefore, although God has given His Word to these suffering slaves to tell them that He is their friend, that He loves them, and that if they believe in Jesus they shall have a home in heaven,—the slaveholders have forbidden them to read it. Five hundred dollars must any Christian man pay in Georgia who teaches a Christian labourer to read the Word of God; and in Louisiana the same act of kindness is felony. So the labourers are crushed. No boa-constrictor ever held an antelope within its coiled folds more tightly than the American slave-holder holds his slave.

By these means the slave-holders, collecting above $200,000,000 annually for themselves, have thereby injured all the other classes.

Slave-hirers have to pay more for the hire of slaves than they would have to pay for the more effective labour of freemen. The mean whites, who form the majority of citizens, are themselves half slaves. Hindered by their poverty from purchasing or hiring slaves, unable to obtain free labour, and too proud to labour themselves, they pass their dishonoured lives in ragged idleness. Hated by the slave for their violence, and hating him for his hatred; despised by the slave-holder for their coarse vulgarity, and hating him for his contempt; but, above all, hating every freeman of the North, because they think him an enemy who would set the slaves free to cut their throats,—they are a most unfortunate, degraded, and unhappy class.

So the slave-holders have been a upas tree, dropping poison over the whole land, and killing all beneath their deadly shadow. Of course they have not escaped themselves. Imperious, passionate, sensual, enemies to all, and suspecting that all are enemies to them, too many of them live in the exercise of boisterous passions which render it impossible for Christian men to feel for them the slightest esteem.

Can then the slave-holder find in his home a garden of roses, when slavery has made his land a volcano where fiery passions have burned up every flower? Not, if his wife sees his image in the slave children growing up around his dwelling; not, if his children, when they curse and rage, tell him that he does these things himself; not, if he is disgraced by their premature depravity; not, if the ferocity by which he makes his slaves tremble renders it impossible that his family should love him.

Yet to extend and to perpetuate this system, by which black men are tormented and white men are debased, is, according to Southern preaching, the mission which God has given the South to discharge. Strange infatuation, if it is not daring blasphemy! God, who would not suffer Israelites to be bondmen, even for a time, because they were His servants, has not ordained that Christians who are His children shall be bondmen for ever. God, who desolated Egypt because the Egyptian slave-holders would hold the Israelites in bondage, is not going to shed His chosen favours upon American slave-holders, because they will keep Christian men and women in a bondage more degrading. Jesus, the Friend of the friendless, has died to ransom the Christian slaves, has welcomed and saved them, (Matt. xii. 28, John vii. 37;) has made them children of God and heirs of heaven, (John i. 12, Rom. viii. 14, 17;) has called them His brothers, (Matt. xii. 49, 50;) and at His return will bless those who were kind to them for His sake, (Matt. xxv. 40.) Does He approve the injustice which tramples on His brothers, and which lashes them to their daily toils? His laws and His example alike condemn it; and when He shall come again arrayed in the splendours of Deity, and attended by the hierarchy of heaven, woe to the men who, under pretence of ownership, oppressed and tormented them! for it is as sure as that He is Judge of quick and dead, that He will say to all such oppressors, though they now lift their heads so proudly, "Inasmuch as ye have done it to one of the least of these my brothers, ye have done it unto me," (Matt. xxv. 40, 45.)

To sustain this system of injustice the slave-holders have rebelled against their government; and when their government and their countrymen armed to put down the rebellion, rather than submit to government and law, they dragged their ignorant fellow-citizens after them into a sanguinary strife; have soaked their fields with human blood; and, accepting Mr Palmer's manifesto, have determined that the last man shall perish behind the last rampart, before they will let the slaves go free. Other causes of strife, such as the tariff, are either imaginary or trivial. This, as their own writers have distinctly shewn, is the great issue—Slave labour for the South, instead of free.

Rather than forego the one or accept the other, they will perish.

In this unprincipled effort to ruin their country rather than emancipate their slaves, let Englishmen never take part. "I tremble for my country," said Jefferson, "when I reflect that God is just, that His justice cannot sleep for ever; that considering numbers and natural means only, a change of situation is among possible events; that it may become probable by supernatural interference. *The Almighty has no attribute which can take side with us in such a contest.*"* So spoke the great slave-holder long ago; and now the contest is come. Sympathy with such oppressors in their rebellion against their lawful government, with a view to perpetuate a cruel tyranny, would be in free England an indelible disgrace. I do not believe that they will ever secure their independence. Mr Jefferson Davis and his brother slave-holders have raised armies only to consume them, and have built iron-clad ships only to blow them up. Instead of making a nation, they are creating a solitude; and when they meant to found an empire, they have been digging a grave. But whether they are to succeed in their undertaking or not, never, at least, let us take one step to secure their independence which would seal the doom of millions who now have the prospect of being free.

Should they ever really secure their independence, Europe must acknowledge it: but to recognise them as

* Jefferson, in Helper, p. 154.

independent, with a view to make them so, just at the moment when their countrymen are forcing them to lay down their arms, would be an insult to a great people, which, if it expired in words, would expose us to universal ridicule; and, if backed by deeds, would be punished by a boundless waste of treasure, and by a deluge of English blood.

No enmity to a nation which contains so many who are brave, generous, and friendly; our allies in the cause of freedom, and our brothers in the kingdom of Christ.

No alliance with the slave-holders against their oppressed labourers.

No interposition between the criminal and justice.

No recognition of Southern independence before it is an accomplished fact.

Should not these be the principles cherished in every English heart, spoken in every family, proclaimed in hundreds of meetings, carried over the land by every mail, till they swell into a voice of thunder, which no statesman can misunderstand? Every man among us who is just and humane, must sympathise with the working-classes of the Slave States; but the working-classes of England should especially feel for them, and I think they do. In almost every meeting, they at least have taken the part of the free North, against the slave-holders of the South. Should the emergency arise when their aid may be required, I trust that hundreds of thousands, in thousands of public meetings, will protest against premature recognition. Premature recognition, as we cannot too often repeat, will be insulting to a friendly nation, impotent to secure its object, disastrous to our finances, and injurious to our reputation. The present Government, who are pledged to neutrality, will be glad to be backed against all external pressure by the voice of the people; and if those of opposite views should come to power, they will be restrained by it from entering upon any opposite course.

CONCLUSION.

The children of God in all parts of the earth are brothers, who have one Father in heaven, and one Saviour, are led by one Spirit, maintain the same great principles, are engaged in promoting the glory of God and the good of man, and after having attained, through grace, perfection in wisdom, holiness, and love, will live eternally together in one happy home. From this similarity in their principles and aims, no less than from the express injunction of the Lord, (John xiii. 34, 35,) they love each other. No country in the world contains more of them than the United States; and there they are distinguished by so many virtues that their brothers in Europe cannot, when their country is bleeding at every pore, but feel the deepest interest in their welfare. For the moment, treason has rent from the United States a territory half the size of Europe, and the slave-holders, grown wanton by long indulgence, are determined to erect it into a hostile slave empire, though hundreds of thousands may perish through the attempt. To sustain their treason, they now ask Europe to recognise their independence. Let the reader bear in mind that, under the government which they wish to ruin, they may have all the liberty which they can desire; and that the slave system which they wish to perpetuate is the most monstrous tyranny which modern times has witnessed. The Tartar government which has placed its iron yoke upon the Chinese, and the Ottoman which rules the Turkish empire with a total disregard of justice, are merciful compared with theirs. Nowhere else in the earth do the rulers of a civilised people buy and sell the labourers of the country, trample on all their domestic ties, work them without pay, substitute the whip for wages, refuse them legal redress for the most intolerable wrongs, exclude them from the courts of justice, and, to reduce them as much as possible to the condition of beasts, make it a crime to teach them to read. A system of such superlative injustice deserves the abhorrence of every good man in the world. God has said to the slave-holder, "Thou shalt love thy neighbour as thyself;" and the slave code says to him, "Thou shalt treat thy neighbour as a beast." The Lord Jesus has said to the slave-holder, with respect to his Christian brother, "A new commandment I give unto you, That ye love one another; as I have loved you, that ye also love one another. By this shall all men know that ye are my disciples, if ye have love one to another." And his brother slave-holders say to him in reply, "Thou shalt treat thy fellow-Christian as a brute without intellect, as a machine without a conscience, as a chattel only made for thy convenience." No language can exaggerate the atrocity of this system, elaborated by able men, and maintained with satanic energy. And now having rebelled against their government, they ask us to reject the friendship of a free and religious people with whom it is an honour and a strength to be allied, that we may lavish our affections, and, if need be, pour out our blood for them. They ask us to secure the triumph of their treason and their tyranny. Appealing to us as if we were the most selfish and the most senseless nation on the earth, they expect us to prefer the trade of six millions of oppressors, who, after a period of lawless expansion, are sure to come to grief, to the good-will of a great people, whose prosperity, based on religion, freedom, and industry, may grow while the world lasts. Will Englishmen listen to them?

Shall we hand it down to our posterity that, using the power which God had given us for better ends to strike down the freeman of the Free States, and the bondman of the Slave States, we dragged the imperial chariot of the slave-holder over the bodies of both? Will Englishmen who broke the chain of the slave in Jamaica rivet it in South Carolina? Will Englishmen sadden the hearts of myriads who do justly, love mercy, and walk humbly with God, that they may receive the plaudits of those whose instruments of government are the cowhide, the manacles, and the revolver; while their national music is formed by the curses of the overseer and the groans of the slave.*

---

* A Southern concert-room is described below:—

"A 'WHIPPING-HOUSE.'—A correspondent of the *Missouri Democrat*, writing from Helena, Arkansas, under date of September 9,

What do the friends of the slave-holders allege to justify their sympathy? "This horrible war is hurrying thousands to the grave for no purpose whatever. The Federal Government can never subdue six millions of freemen, who are masters of such a territory, and

describes as follows one of the beauties of the 'peculiar institution:'—

"'Perhaps your readers are not aware that whipping negroes is a regular business in some parts of the South; but such is undoubtedly the case. Improved machinery has been invented and put into operation, and whipping is done by wholesale.

"'An institution of this kind is located at Mayena, twenty-five miles from this place, on the St Francis Road. The "whipping-house," as it is called, is about six feet in diameter and ten feet high. A shaft runs from bottom to top; on the upper end is a small cog-wheel running horizontally, into which a large wheel works. The propelling power is a robust negro. Attached to the shaft are leather thongs or straps about two inches wide. Lashes are inserted in these, and when the shaft is in motion they reach the neck. Near by is the office and stripping-house. Here the victims are divested of their clothing, and five or six are placed in the torture-room; the door being fastened, the negro on hold of the crank, the proprietor, with watch in hand, orders the machine to be put in motion.

"'Around whirls the shaft, at the rate of two hundred revolutions per minute, with straps and lashes extended, bruising and lacerating the poor victim with thousands of blows extending from head to foot. Fifteen minutes is considered by the proprietor, Hampton Jones, to be a reasonable time to grind a batch of human flesh; and then it is so very cheap, costing but a dollar per head! I do think it very nearly equals hell itself. Nothing for human torture could be more terrible. A thousand scorpions stinging their flesh could not inflict more punishment. At the end of the time, the poor, bleeding, quivering victims are brought out more dead than alive. The plantations for miles send their grists to this mill to be ground, and the proprietor had been doing a thriving business until the Union troops came.'"—*Daily News*, December 15.

who are determined to be independent. We are friends to the North, as well as to the South, when we propose a friendly mediation through which each may concede so much to the other as may form the basis of an honourable peace. In the interests of humanity let us try to stop this barbarous, brutalising, fratricidal, atrocious, inhuman, fiendish, and eternal war."

To render the proposal plausible, we must ascertain if the combatants wish for any mediation; and if so, who is to be the mediator, and what are to be the terms proposed.

If you do not mean to use force, what is the use of offering a mediation which both the combatants are resolved not to accept. If any change of circumstances should render them more ready to accept such an offer, the Government which mediates must be one which is believed by both parties to be friendly, because no one will put his affairs for arbitration into the hands of his enemy. If this be true, we, however we may flatter ourselves, are not the country to mediate, for neither the Federals nor the Confederates believe us to be friendly to them. Although those who are zealous for mediation are partisans of the South, who openly express their wishes for its complete success, yet the slave-holders do not believe us as a nation to be their friends. On the contrary, they hate us as abolitionists, and they believe us to wish their humiliation.

Still less is our mediation likely to be acceptable to the Federals. Our Government has been sincerely neutral; but various considerations have led them to suppose that it is unfriendly. The early recognition of the rebels as a belligerent power has been understood by them as an expression of hostility; a leading member of the Government, overlooking the great interests for which they are contending,—their nationality, their territory, their commerce, their future peace, their safety,—has declared that they are fighting for empire. This has naturally been understood by them to mean that they are prompted by a lawless lust of aggrandisement, as we should be if we went to war for the acquisition of Greece and Egypt; or as France would be if she should fight to extend her frontiers to the Rhine; or Russia, if she were to annex the Turkish empire. Another member has expressed his opinion of the power and prowess of the South on insufficient evidence in such terms as to make the Americans believe that the wish was father to the thought. Other things have strengthened their conviction that our Government, though neutral in policy, is not neutral in its sympathies. The *Alabama*, a vessel of war, built in an English dock, armed with English guns, and manned chiefly by English sailors, is capturing and burning every American merchantman which it can find, not always sparing, if report speaks true, even English vessels with the English flag. To this we must add, that if the offer of mediation is made by our Government, it will be in deference to the enemies of the United States, who loudly demand it, and against the wishes of their friends, who believe that they have both the right and the power to put down the rebellion. As a matter of fact, many of the Democratic party, who are zealously supported by our sympathisers with the South, are so irritated against us, that in a large Democratic meeting lately held in New York, hopes were expressed that the North and the South would again be united in order to attack England.* In such a temper, both the Confederates and the Federals would reject the mediation of a country which both parties believe to be unfriendly to them.

No proposals from a mediator so suspected could be favourably received. But if our relations with the two belligerents were cordial, if we could be equally fair and friendly to the government and to the rebels, to the liberators of the slave and to the slave-holders, so that both parties could trust us, what terms have we to propose? Omitting details, which, however, involve endless difficulties, it has been proposed to establish peace on the condition that the slave-holders shall keep their slaves, with all the territory lying between the Potomac and the Mississippi. Hateful as this would be to both parties, who would at once repudiate it, it would, unless we have forgotten all our efforts to liberate the slaves, be supremely odious to England. According to it, Englishmen are to prolong by their counsels the bondage of four millions of our race, many of them our brothers and sisters in Christ, just when, by the justice and the mercy of their national government, they are about to enjoy their freedom. English mediation is to consign them to unpaid toils, to merci-

* *Daily News*, December 11.

less punishment, to unalleviated misery, when their hearts are beating with the hopes of wages, of family ties, of the protection of law, and of a free access to the Word of God.

Could we hear again the anti-slavery eloquence of Wilberforce, whose very anger was benevolent, and whose genial temper conciliated his bitterest opponents; could Fowell Buxton stand once more among us, with his imperturbable firmness in the cause of humanity; could the vigorous pen of Stephen be again wielded in the battle of freedom; or could Zachary Macaulay bring again to the same cause his strong, clear intellect, his hearty zeal, and his indefatigable perseverance, they would cry out, "Shame, shame!" to us, their degenerate successors, who aid the American slave-holder to rivet the fetters of his slave.

Terms less distasteful to Europe, but not less unfair to the United States, have been advocated both in France and England. According to these, the Federal Government is to acknowledge the independence of the Slave States, and the Slave States are to emancipate their slaves.

If this is all that diplomatic wisdom can devise, we may be sure that North and South will alike scorn our interference.

Never will the United States consent to be dismembered, impoverished, endangered, humiliated by the triumph of the rebellion, while they have any power left to prevent it. And never will the slave-holders accept emancipation, which they believe to be humiliation, poverty, disgrace, and expatriation, till they are absolutely crushed. The offer of such terms would be accepted as a mortal injury by the slave-holders, because, as they have repeatedly told us, to live with their enfranchised slaves would be so loathsome to them that they will rather die than make the experiment; and the United States would no less resent it, because they believe fully that they can, with the blessing of God, extinguish the rebellion. Such mediation, sure as it is beforehand to be rejected, would only exasperate the combatants by increasing the fear of emancipation in the one party, and of Southern independence in the other; while we should justly reap the world's ridicule for exposing ourselves by stupid propositions to a contemptuous refusal.

Some would give effect to our mediation by attaching to it a recognition of the independence of the South, without any armed intervention. A deliberate judgment pronounced by our Government, that the South ought to be independent, might, as they think, arrest the slaughter which is hurrying so many victims to an untimely end. Our Government is asked to recognise the South, not because the war is at an end, but because it is raging,—not because the South is independent, but to make it so.

On this supposition, we are called to erect by our moral influence a great slave power which might otherwise be compelled to relinquish its injustice. Never did a free nation bring so black a stain upon its character as we should upon ours if this policy should

P

prevail. We should thus stultify all the efforts which we have hitherto made to abolish slavery,—we should be apostates from the generous sentiments which have done us some honour in the world,—we should inflict the greatest wrong upon many of our fellow-Christians, in both sections of the United States,—and we should do the greatest dishonour to our Saviour Christ. There are, I trust, sufficient numbers of conscientious men in this country to shield us by their protests from this great crime.

Even those who, like a certain French writer, think that a blunder is worse than a crime, should on that account oppose this recognition of a fictitious independence. The slave-holder will of course fight more desperately, because encouraged by our good wishes, and looking for more substantial proofs of our regard. But, on the other hand, the Federal Government would take good care that the recognised independence should never pass from a fiction into a fact. Our premature recognition, instead of creating the independence, would prevent it, and after loading us with the world's derision, because we were so dull as to mistake imaginations for realities, leave to our children an inheritance of enduring American resentment for no purpose whatsoever.

If we recognise the independence of the South, we must act accordingly, by breaking the blockade, and by re-opening the cotton trade. That, the United States would resist, and we should have war. "Then let us have war," say some. "Recognition, with an armed intervention, will soon force them to abandon this unnatural and monstrous attempt to bring so many millions who are now become a nation under their yoke."

On this point let us hear Mr Frederick Douglass, a liberated slave. After stating that we have freed 800,000 slaves in the West Indies, and that he had been himself ransomed by some friends in England, he thus continues:—

"I am grateful for your benevolence, jealous for your honour, but chiefly now I am concerned, lest, in the present tremendous crisis of American affairs, you should be led to adopt a policy which may defeat the now proposed emancipation of my people, and forge new fetters of slavery for unborn millions of their posterity. You are now more than ever urged, both from within and from without your borders, to recognise the independence of the so-called Confederate States of America. I beseech and implore you, resist this urgency. You have nobly resisted it thus long. You can, and I ardently hope you will, resist it still longer. The proclamation of emancipation by President Lincoln will become operative on the first day of January 1863. The hopes of millions, long trodden down, now rise with every advancing hour. Oh! I pray you, by all your highest and holiest memories, blast not the budding hopes of these millions by lending your countenance and extending your potent and honoured hand to the blood-stained fingers of the slave-holding Confederate States of America.

"For the honour of the British name, which has

hitherto carried only light and hope to the slave, and rebuke and dismay to the slave-holder, do not in this great emergency be persuaded to abandon and contradict that policy of justice and mercy to the negro which has made your character revered, and your name illustrious, throughout the civilised world. Your enemies even have been compelled to respect the sincerity of your philanthropy. Would you retain this respect, welcome not those human fleshmongers, those brokers in the bodies and souls of men, who have dared to knock at your doors for admission into the family of nations. Their pretended government is but a foul conspiracy against the sacred rights of mankind, and does not deserve the name of government. Its foundation is laid in the dogma that man may rightfully hold property in man, and flog him to toil like a beast of burden. Have no fellowship, I pray you, with these merciless men-stealers.

"Your noblest sons, living and dead, have taught the world to loathe and abhor slavery as the vilest of modern abominations. You have sacrificed millions of pounds and thousands of lives to arrest and put an end to the piratical slave-traffic on the coast of Africa; and will you now, when the light of your best teachings is finding its way to the darkest corners of the earth, and men are beginning to adopt and practically carry out your benevolent ideas,—will you now, in such a time, utterly dishonour your high example and your long-cherished principles? Can you, at the bidding or importunity of those negro-driving lords of the lash, whose wealth is composed of the wages of labourers which they have kept back by fraud and force, take upon you and your children the dreadful responsibility of arresting the arm now outstretched to break the chains of the American slave?

"Can it be doubted that the hope so persistently kept alive by such organs of British public opinion as the London *Times*, and by such eminent statesmen as Mr Gladstone, that recognition of the independence of the Confederate States is only a question of time,—that this hope is one grand source of the strength of our slave-holding rebellion? Your early concession of belligerent rights to the rebels—the adoption of neutrality as between the loyal and the rebel governments—the oft-repeated assertion in high places that the rebels can never be subdued—the ill-concealed exultation sometimes witnessed over disasters to our arms—with much else which it can do no good and might do harm to mention here,—have evidently served the bad purpose of keeping life and spirit in this horrible rebellion.

"I have no hesitation in saying that if you, Great Britain, had, at the outset of this terrible war, sternly frowned upon the conspirators, and had given your earnest and unanimous sympathy and moral support to the loyal cause, to-day might have seen America enjoying peace and security, and you would not have been the sufferer in all your commercial and manufacturing interests you now are. The misfortune is that your rebukes of the North have been construed into sympathy and approval at the South. Your good opinion of the slave-holders has been taken as a renunciation of your former abhorrence of slavery; and you have thus kept these Confederate slave-masters in countenance from the beginning.

"The whole history of the rebellion will shew that the slave-holding rebels revolted, not because of any violation of the United States Constitution, or of any proposed violation of it, but from pure and simple opposition to the Constitution itself, and because, in their judgment, that Constitution does not sufficiently guard and protect slavery. Wanting a slave constitution, from which all hope of emancipation should be excluded, the Southern States have undertaken to make one, and to establish it upon the ruins of the old one, under which slavery could be discouraged, crippled, and abolished. The war, therefore, to maintain the old against the new constitution is essentially an anti-slavery war.

"You are unable to obtain your usual supply of American cotton. Would this be made better by plunging yourselves into the hardships, expenses, horrors, and perils of a war, which would in any event shed no lustre on your arms, and only feed the fires of national hate for a century to come, and just in this your time of need greatly diminish your American supply of corn? Can any thinking man doubt for one moment that intervention would be an aggravation rather than a mitigation of the evils under which your labourers mourn? It is insisted that you ought, from considerations of humanity toward both sections, intervene, and put an end to the fratricidal strife. Could you put an end to it? Never did wilder delusion beset a human brain. I say it in no menacing spirit, the United States, though wounded and bleeding, is yet powerful. Heavy as have been her losses, in life and treasure, her weaknesses from these causes offer no temptation to foreign assault.

"No excuses, however plausible—no distances of time, however remote—no line of conduct hereafter pursued, however excellent—will erase the deep stain upon your honour and truth, if, at this hour of dreadful trial, you interpose in a manner to defeat or embarrass the emancipation of the slaves of America."

There are many good reasons why we should not engage in this quarrel. In the first place, it is no business of ours. If we are to fight for the independence of every disaffected portion of every empire, we shall have plenty of work on our hands. Why should we not at once send out an army and fleet to secure the independence of the Tae-Pings? They are not six millions, as the Confederates, but thirty millions; they are not, like the slave-holders, opposed to a government wielding forces greatly superior to their own, but to an effete despotism; and the war in which they are engaged is in its details barbarous and revolting. If we engage in war to rescue the slave-holders from the punishment of their rebellion, how much more should we fight for the Tae-Pings! This war is no business of ours. The United States have done us no wrong; and we have no right to break up their country into fragments, to lessen their wealth, dignity, and power, to destroy their future peace, and to endanger their liberty, that we may gratify a few rebellious oligarchs. God has given us no commission to drive our bullets or our bayonets through the bodies of men whose only crime is defending their country from the fatal effects of rebellion. Patriotic, estimable, and godly young soldiers from Connecticut or Massachusetts, lying on the wet or frosty ground, with their limbs broken, their flesh mangled, and their life-blood flowing fast through their wounds, would, like Stephen, say of their murderers, "Lord, lay not this sin to their charge;" but could their prayer be heard? Brave young Englishmen, too, stricken down in a quarrel in which all their best feelings would be on the side of the enemy, would in their death-agony mingle their thoughts of distant homes which they must never see more, with the reflection that they had fallen in the attempt to destroy those who had been sent out to defend the best interests of their country. This horrid slaughter would involve many victims. Probably not less than one hundred thousand of the allies, and more than seven hundred thousand Russians, perished in the Crimean war; and the men whom we should have to meet on the other side the Atlantic, are not serfs forced into the army by conscription, and fighting under the obligation of military discipline; but patriots who, with Anglo-Saxon courage, have also a knowledge that the highest interests of their country compel them to an energetic perseverance.

The authors of such a war would also have to charge themselves with an extravagant waste of public money. If the allied powers could not compel the Czar to open the gates of Sebastopol at a less cost than a hundred millions of money, let no one fancy that a war with the United States to give independence to the slave-holders would cost us less. The Americans have at this moment eight armies in the field; besides their wooden navy, they have forty iron-cased vessels; forty gunboats also heavily armed are about to open the Mississippi from New Orleans to St Louis; and the whole Federal naval force consists of three hundred and twenty-three steamers, and one hundred and four sailing vessels, carrying in all three thousand two hundred and sixty-eight guns.* Twenty millions of men, who have sent eight hundred thousand soldiers into the field, are united as one man to defend themselves against the lawless slave-holders; and will they manifest less energy than the Russians did? This unnatural war between us and them, if ever it takes place, will add at least a hundred millions to our burdens. Our working-classes, not too rich now, must be further taxed, that our armies and fleets may inflict the greatest possible mischief upon the working-classes of the Free States and of the Slave States. Seventy millions per annum in a time of peace is not enough, but we must pay a hundred millions more to make the slave-holder independent, and to destroy the hopes of his labourers. That sum would be penalty enough for this outrageous

* Report of the Secretary of the Navy; *Daily News*, Dec. 16.

intermeddling, but that would ill represent our loss. If we are ever pushed by hatred and passion into this war, we shall have to fight our best customer, that we may gratify the pride of our worst. A few slave-holders ruling over a multitude of ragged whites, and of slaves who cannot call their limbs their own, will never do us much good. The slaveless whites have no money to spend on foreign goods, and the slave-holders take care that the slaves shall have none. By this war we should therefore ruin a great trade that we may raise one which must at best be contemptibly small. To this loss we must add the capture of our merchantmen, whom our magnificent *Warriors* would be ill able to protect from the swift, small iron-clads which would soon swarm upon the ocean, picking up our traders in every latitude, and making London and Liverpool rue the day when we provoked into hostile activity an energy at least equal to our own. Let us remember, that if we engage in this war, which will be to them an act of necessary self-defence, they will go to the extent of national bankruptcy rather than not beat us. If their forty gunboats and their forty iron-cased vessels are not enough to sink our fleets in their harbours, they will soon launch eighty more; if their four hundred vessels of war are not enough to play havoc with our commerce, they will build and arm four hundred more; if seven hundred thousand men in arms could not drive us into the sea, they will enlist and drill seven hundred thousand more. Meanwhile, exasperated by our malicious intervention, they would dash with such impetuosity into the rebel territory that not a bale of cotton could escape their raids; and, forbidding a single cargo of wheat to leave their shores, they would add to the cotton famine a scarcity of food, which will soon make all the working-classes of England suffer for our support of the slave-holder.

Are we sure how this cost would end? If by our wasteful zeal in a bad cause we could take possession of the Southern seaports, lay New York and Boston in ashes, block up the Mississippi, and make the whole coast feel the effects of our fierce Vandalism, they would bear ten times more than that before they would sue for peace. Could we then follow them into the interior, far from our supplies, with an energetic, intelligent population in mass swarming round our ill-fated regiments, and harassing them day and night? If not, no efforts of ours can make them ruin their country by acknowledging the independence of the slave-holders.

If such a war shall occur, it will indeed be well if it does not end in our shameful defeat. Their iron-clad navy, though not constructed for the open sea, is fully equal within their harbours to any naval force which we can send against them; and their armies will far outnumber ours. They will have command of all the resources of their vast country, and the advantages possessed by those who have to defend rather than to attack; and they will meet a cold sense of the obligation to fight in our troops by an enthusiastic ardour to protect their families from an unprincipled invasion. But, beyond this, it ought not to surprise us if we find that our men contract such a disgust at the service as to refuse to fight,—not from fear, but from conscience,—not because they are careless of their country's glory, but because they cannot bear to be the agents of its disgrace. When they shall march through the smiling villages of Connecticut and Massachusetts, bringing fire and sword to a people whose only fault is that they have fought to suppress a wicked rebellion, the moral sense of Englishmen may be stronger than military obedience, and they may fraternise with those whom we sent them out to murder.

Should France consent to aid us in this unholy crusade against law and liberty, that alliance would be still more dastardly. When all the energies of a free Protestant people are tasked to the utmost to subdue a lawless conspiracy, we are to join with France to assist the conspirators. Because that nation finds it hard to preserve its integrity against the fury and fanaticism of the rebels, we will try what two armies and two navies from the most powerful nations of the world can do for its dismemberment. We will seize the favourable moment of its great agony to break it to pieces. Two stout men meeting another with his hands tied, flourish their sticks, and cry, "Come on! come on!" We see a neighbour grappling with assassins, and run up to plunge our knives into his breast. Every generous man in the world would call it cowardly and base. But even so we should not succeed. Could France and England occupy New York as Napoleon occupied Moscow, the Americans would retire from their seaports, as the Russians from the blazing Kremlin, only to defy the utmost efforts of their assailants.

Above all, it is impossible that God should not behold such injustice with anger; and if He take part against us, the forces of nature which are under His command, and the course of events which is shaped by His providence, may soon convince us how unwise it is to boast of wealth, skill, or valour in a cause upon which it is impossible without impiety to ask His blessing.

But come what will, our attempts to crush the labouring classes of the South, by upholding their oppressors, must entail on us eternal infamy. History will transmit the memory of this crime to distant generations. Stripped of all the disguises by which we now attempt to veil its deformity, it will stand out in its naked ugliness. Vice must ever put on the mask of virtue, or it could not lead the multitude; but the merciless veracity of the historian will explode the vain pretences by which we now seek to glorify the support of lawlessness and tyranny. State sovereignty, the constitutional right of secession, the tyranny of the American majority, the chivalry of the glorious seceders, their patriarchal tenderness to their slaves, the certainty that they would when independent emancipate them, the impossibility of a reunion of the North and South, from their opposite natures and their incompatible interests,—all these and other imaginations will have vanished like the baseless fabric of a vision. Then it will be recorded how, when the

Americans honoured our Queen, we vilified their President,—when they proffered us friendship, we bade them take our enmity instead,—when they armed to put down rebellion, we called it ferocity,—when they took measures to emancipate the slave, we stigmatised it as hypocrisy. Pretending to sicken at the sight of blood, we proceeded to shed it in torrents. Compassionating the sufferers in Lancashire, we first prolonged the cotton famine, then added a scarcity of food, and then loaded the people with new burdens by a useless war. Like the slave-holders, we were so proud of our liberty, that we could not bear that others should be free. The energy, intelligence, and virtue of the American people, which ought to have commanded our esteem, only inspired us with jealousy, and we sacrificed men and money without stint to break them into fragments, because we dreaded that their unity would render them a greater people than ourselves. The freest nation of the East, we strove to ruin the freest nation of the West, and were so enamoured of the slave-holder, who was at once a rebel and a tyrant, that we waded through a sea of blood, and marched over piles of the dying and the dead to give victory to his standard, and to render his slave-power perpetual.

Such will be the verdict of posterity if the wishes of a few should hurry us into a support of the slave-holders' rebellion.

But Englishmen will never be so misled; nor, while our present rulers hold the helm, will the Government attempt to mislead them. It is matter of just satisfaction that it rejected the late proposal of the French Emperor.

If the object of the proposed mediation was to secure, by the influence of France and England, an armistice of six months, and then the independence of the South, the proposal of it was an act of hostility to the United States. Let us remember what is involved in their acknowledgment of this independence. They would thus render abortive the cost and sufferings of this terrible war; they must avow themselves defeated by those who have not one-third of their numbers. Treason will then triumph, their country will be dismembered, a hostile slave empire will be established at their doors, new secessions will follow, they will lose their place among the nations, and be the laughing-stock of their enemies all over the world. To all this they are called to submit when the magnitude of their fleets and armies, their inexhaustible resources, their ardent patriotism, and the oneness of the two great political parties in their resolution to prosecute the war, render it probable, if God bless their efforts, that they will speedily extinguish the rebellion. They will see, I trust, from this decision that our Government is not less friendly than the French, and is perfectly sincere in its resolution to maintain an honourable neutrality. From our journals and from public meetings they may further learn that in this the nation is of one mind with the Government; and will sustain it against the few who wish by mediation to secure recognition, and by recognition war.

But is not the time come when our Government, drawing after it the other Governments of Europe, may counsel the Confederates to lay down their arms? Could Mr Jefferson Davis and his colleagues completely triumph, the confederacy would not deserve recognition because the eleven revolted States are too weak to be recognised as eleven nations; and eleven sovereign and independent States which declare themselves to be distinct nations, and may separate legally any day, can never form one nation. Mr Davis can, therefore, neither make them into eleven nations nor into one. Beaten in battle, he may indeed organise a guerilla system of plunder and murder which may reduce the States in which it prevails to anarchy and barbarism; but this will secure no victory over the national government, and will probably so harass and disgust the Slave States themselves that they would rise in mass against the brigands. Anything else is becoming impossible to him. His men and his means seem to be nearly exhausted: his men, or he would not be obliged to extend his conscription from the age of thirty-five to forty-five; and his means, or he would not have left his main army to fight without shoes or decent clothes. The slaveless majority must soon be weary of a strife which if successful brings them no advantage, and if disastrous will inflict upon them hardships, disease, mutilation, and early death; and the negroes are beginning to be free. The Eleven States, like a drove of Virginian slaves destined for the Western market, are bound together by two cords—the slave-system, and the war; while the great trader and his colleagues ride behind well armed to prevent their escape. But each of the eleven knows that he has a right to be free, and, despite cords, whips, and revolvers, any one may, any hour, slip away, leaving the drove and its drivers to their fate.

On the other hand, the military power of the United States has been growing rapidly. Two years ago, when the war began, they had not one army, now they have eight; then they had no iron-cased vessels, they have now forty-one; then their whole navy was small, now it numbers 427 vessels with 3268 guns; then all their fighting men by sea and land were less than twenty thousand, they are now above 700,000, resolved to save their country or perish. Their President is a firm, upright, patriotic man, beloved by all who can love goodness; Republicans and Democrats alike are determined to suppress the rebellion; Christians by tens of thousands in that land are praying for their country; and, with the blessing of God, it will be soon triumphant.

If the Governments of Europe are anxious to prevent the effusion of blood, let them warn the slaveholders that their cause is as hopeless as it is criminal. Predictions of their success, and proposals to recognise them, can only stimulate them to desperate obstinacy, and load their fields with useless carnage; but if Europe will urge them to accept emancipation as inevitable, and to return to their allegiance, the war may cease. It is no disgrace to be beaten by the Federals, who are three times more numerous than they. They can scarcely hope to retain their labourers in bondage, because they are now legally free; submission is only a return to duty; and they will be far happier as landowners with a thriving tenantry and with contented labourers, than they have been as the guardians of a system which they could only maintain by burning men alive. A strong remonstrance from Europe would enable them to yield with all the better grace, and would save the lives of myriads.

But if the Governments of Europe will not go beyond neutrality, men of faith may accomplish by prayer what ministers of state will not attempt by diplomacy. God who has all hearts at His disposal has directed us specially to pray for those in power, (1 Tim. ii. 1–4;) and if His servants in Europe unite with those of America in earnest supplication, He may liberate the oppressed negroes, and, disposing the slave-holders to dutiful allegiance, may lead their countrymen generously to forgive their fault: thus the two sections of the country, freed from their only cause of quarrel, may be formed into a peaceful, homogeneous people; which may spread over their great continent as one of the freest, most virtuous, and happiest nations on the earth.

THE END.

www.ingramcontent.com/pod-product-compliance
Lightning Source LLC
Chambersburg PA
CBHW031354230426
43670CB00006B/537